RIPPED OUT OF THE BIBLE

Whosoever therefore shall be ashamed of me
and of my words
in this adulterous and sinful generation;
of him also shall the Son of man be ashamed,
when he cometh in the glory of his Father
with the holy angels.

Mark 8:38

Twelfth Edition – 2019
Revised, Enlarged, & Reformatted

FLOYD NOLEN JONES, Th.D., Ph.D.

Global Evangelism INC
15 King David Dr.
Jackson, TN 38305
C.jacobs@actsforlife.com

For more information, phone: 877-KJBIBLE

Ripped out of the Bible

Floyd Jones Ministries, Inc.

TABLE OF CONTENTS

ABBREVIATIONS

A.D.	*Anno Dei* (Year of God)
א	Codex *Sinaiticus* – pronounced *aleph*, the 1st letter in the Hebrew alphabet
B	Codex *Vaticanus*
c.	*circa* – about; approximately
ch.,chs.	chapter(s)
cp.	compare
d.	died
ed., eds.	edition(s); editor(s)
e.g.	*exempli gratia* – for example
etc.	*et cetera* – and so forth
fn.	footnote
ibid.	*ibidem* – Latin for "in the same place"
i.e.	*id est* – that is
KJB/KJ	King James Bible (1611)
LXX	Septuagint, for the "70" (72) translators
mss	Greek ms of New Testament in small cursive letters. Also called "minuscules".
MSS	Greek MSS or Codex of the New Testament written in capital letters. Also called "majuscules" and "uncials".
MS/ms	A single uncial or cursive manuscript.
NASV	New American Standard Version (Bible) – also shortened to NAS
Nestle[26]	The 26th edition of Nestle's Greek N.T. (same as Nestle-Aland[26] or Aland-Nestle[26])
NIV	New International Version
NT	New Testament
op. cit.	*opere citato* – Latin for "in the work previously cited"
OT	Old Testament
p., pp.	page(s)
rev.	revision; revised; revised; reviewed by
TR	*Textus Receptus* – the "Received Text". The Providentially preserved God given Greek N.T. Synonymous, for practical purposes, with "Traditional Text", "Syrian Text", "Byzantine", and "majority text" – although this is a simplification.
T.T.	Traditional Text – a text representing the "vast majority of authorities"
UBS[3]	United Bible Society, 3rd edition of its Greek N.T.
Vid. supra	*Vide supra* – see above; previous pages or materials in the book that one is reading.
vol., vols.	volume(s)

Section A
Key Passages Missing

The first list is a sampling depicting omissions that are commonplace in modern versions.[1] **These omissions often diminish basic doctrines.** The New International Version, which we have used as a representative, has somewhat fewer omissions than the New American Standard, Revised Standard, New English, etc. Yet even in the NIV, the deletions are considerable and noteworthy. This will become increasingly evident as the reader continues farther into this manuscript.

The two translations have been placed side by side so that the earnest inquirer can readily perceive the magnitude of the situation and determine for himself whether the NIV has the same authority and reverence as the Authorized Version. None of the boldfaced/underlined words in that which follows appear in the NIV text (1978 edition, as to just how untrustworthy the NIV is as a translation, see page 52).

King James Bible	New International Version
MAT 1:25 And knew her not till she had brought forth her **firstborn** son...	But he had no union with her until she gave birth to a son.
MAT 5:44 But I say unto you, Love your enemies, **bless them that curse you, do good to them that hate you, and pray for them which despitefully use you,** and persecute you;	But I tell you: Love your enemies and pray for those who persecute you.
MAT 6:13 And lead us not into temptation, but deliver us from evil: **For thine is the kingdom, and the power, and the glory, for ever. Amen.**	And lead us not into temptation but deliver us from the evil one.

---

[1] Most of the material in sections A-E has been adapted by permission from Dr. Jack A. Moorman's excellent manuscript, *Missing in Modern Bibles*, (Collingswood, NJ: Bible For Today Press, #1726, 1989), pp. 3 – 41.

MAT 9:13 ...for I am not come to call the righteous, but sinners **to repentance.**

...For I have not come to call the righteous but sinners.

MAT 15:8 This people **draweth nigh unto me with their mouth,** and honoureth me with their lips; but their heart is far from me.

These people honour me with their lips, but their hearts are far from me.

MAT 16:3 ...**O ye hypocrites,** ye can discern the face of the sky; but can ye not discern the signs of the times?

You know how to interpret the appearance of the sky, but you cannot interpret the signs of the times.

MAT 17:21 **Howbeit this kind goeth not out but by prayer and fasting.**

———

MAT 19:9 And I say unto you, Whosoever shall put away his wife, except it be for fornication, and shall marry another, committeth adultery: **and whoso marrieth her which is put away doth commit adultery.**

I tell you that anyone who divorces his wife, except for marital unfaithfulness and marries another woman commits adultery.

MAT 20:16 So the last shall be first and the first last: **for many be called but few chosen.**

So the last will be first, and the first will be last.

MAT 20:22 But Jesus answered and said, Ye know not what ye ask. Are ye able to drink of the cup that I shall drink of, **and to be baptized with the baptism that I am baptized with?**...

You don't know what you are asking, Jesus said to them. Can you drink the cup I am going to drink?

MAT 23:14 **Woe unto you, scribes and Pharisees, hypocrites! for ye devour widows' houses, and for a pretence make long prayer: therefore ye shall receive the greater damnation.**

———

MAT 27:35 And they crucified him, and parted his garments, casting lots: **that it might be fulfilled which was spoken by the prophet, They parted my garments among them, and upon my vesture did they cast lots.**

When they had crucified him, they divided up his clothes by casting lots.

MAT 28:2 ...for the angel of the Lord descended from heaven, and came and rolled back the stone **from the door,** and sat upon it.

...for an angel of the Lord came down from heaven and going to the tomb, rolled back the stone and sat on it.

MAT 28:9 **And as they went to tell his disciples,** behold, Jesus met them, saying, All hail...

Suddenly Jesus met them. "Greetings," he said...

MK 1:14 Now after that John was put in prison, Jesus came into Galilee, preaching the gospel **of the kingdom** of God.

After John was put in prison, Jesus went into Galilee, proclaiming the good news of God.

MK 1:31 And he came and took her by the hand, and lifted her up; and **immediately** the fever left her.

So he went to her, took her hand and helped her up. The fever left her.

MK 2:17 ...I came not to call the righteous, but sinners **to repentance.**

...I have not come to call the righteous, but sinners.

MK 6:11 ...shake off the dust under your feet for a testimony against them. **Verily I say unto you, it shall be more tolerable for Sodom and Gomorrha in the day of judgment than for that city.**

...shake the dust off your feet when you leave, as a testimony against them.

MK 7:8 For laying aside the commandment of God, ye hold the tradition of men, **as the washing of pots and cups: and many other such like things ye do.**

Ye have let go of the commands of God and are holding on to the traditions of men.

MK 7:16 **If any man have ears to hear, let him hear.**

_____

MK 9:44 **Where their worm dieth not, and the fire is not quenched.**

———

MK 9:46 **Where their worm dieth not, and the fire is not quenched.**

———

MK 9:49 For every one shall be salted with fire, **and every sacrifice shall be salted with salt.**

Everyone will be salted with fire.

MK 10:21 ...and give to the poor, and thou shalt have treasure in heaven: and come, **take up the cross,** and follow me.

...give to the poor, and you will have treasure in heaven. Then come, follow me.

MK 10:24 ...Children, how hard is it **for them that trust in riches** to enter into the kingdom of God.

...Children, how hard it is to enter the kingdom of God.

MK 11:26 **But if ye do not forgive, neither will your Father which is in heaven forgive your trespasses.**

———

MK 13:14 But when ye shall see the abomination of desolation, **spoken of by Daniel the prophet,** standing where it ought not,...

When you see the abomination that causes desolation standing where it does not belong,

MK 13:33 Take ye heed, watch **and pray:** for ye know not when the time is.

Be on guard! Be alert! You do not know when that time will come.

MK 14:68 But he denied, saying, I know not, neither understand I what thou sayest. And he went out into the porch; **and the cock crew.**

But he denied it. "I don't know or understand what you're talking about." he said, and went out into the entryway.

MK 15:28 **And the scripture was fulfilled which saith, And he was numbered with the transgressors.**

———

LUK 1:28 And the angel came in unto her, and said, Hail, thou that art highly favoured, the Lord is with thee: **blessed art thou among women.**

The angel went to her and said, "Greetings, you who are highly favored! The Lord is with you."

LUK 2:43 And when they had fulfilled the days, as they returned, the child Jesus tarried behind in Jerusalem; and **Joseph and his mother** knew not of it.

After the Feast was over, while his parents were returning home, the boy Jesus stayed behind in Jerusalem, but they were unaware of it.

LUK 4:8 And Jesus answered **and said unto him, Get thee behind me, Satan:** for it is written, Thou shalt worship the Lord thy God, and him only shalt thou serve.

Jesus answered, "It is written: 'Worship the Lord your God and serve him only.' "

LUK 9:54 And when his disciples James and John saw this, they said, Lord, wilt thou that we command fire to come down from heaven, and consume them, **even as Elias did?**

When the disciples James and John saw this, they asked, "Lord, do you want us to call fire down from heaven to destroy them?"

LUK 9:55 But he turned, and rebuked them, **and said, Ye know not what manner of spirit ye are of.**

But Jesus turned and rebuked them.

LUK 11:2–4 ...When ye pray, say, **Our** Father **which art in heaven,** Hallowed be thy name. Thy kingdom come. **Thy will be done, as in heaven, so in earth.** Give us day by day our daily bread. And forgive us our sins; for we also forgive every one that is indebted to us. And lead us not into temptation; **but deliver us from evil.**

When you pray, say: Father hallowed be your name, your kingdom come. Give us each day our daily bread. Forgive us our sins, for we also forgive everyone who sins against us. And lead us not into temptation.

LUK 11:29 ...This is an evil generation: they seek a sign; and there shall no sign be given it, but the sign of Jonas **the prophet.**

...This is a wicked generation. It asks for a miraculous sign, but none will be given it except the sign of Jonah.

LUK 17:36 **Two men shall be in the field; the one shall be taken, and the other left.**

———

LUK 22:31 **And the Lord said,** Simon, Simon, behold, Satan **hath desired to have you,** that he may sift you as wheat.

Simon, Simon, Satan has asked to sift you as wheat.

LUK 22:64 And when they had blindfolded him, **they struck him on the face,** and asked him, saying, Prophesy, who is it that smote thee?

They blindfolded him and demanded, "Prophesy! Who hit you?"

LUK 23:17 **(For of necessity he must release one unto them at the feast.)**

———

LUK 23:38 And a superscription also was written over him **in letters of Greek, and Latin, and Hebrew,** THIS IS THE KING OF THE JEWS.

There was a written notice above him, which read: THIS IS THE KING OF THE JEWS.

JOH 1:27 He it is, who coming after me **is preferred before me,** whose shoe's latchet I am not worthy to unloose.

He is the one who comes after me, the thongs of whose sandals I am not worthy to untie.

JOH 3:13 And no man hath ascended up to heaven, but he that came down from heaven, even the Son of man **which is in heaven.**

No one has ever gone into heaven except the one who came from heaven the Son of man.

JOH 5:3–4 In these lay a great multitude of impotent folk, of blind, halt, withered, **waiting for the moving of the water. For an angel went down at a certain season into the pool, and troubled the water: whosoever then first after the troubling of the water stepped in was made whole of whatsoever disease he had.**

Here a great number of disabled people used to lie – the blind, the lame, the paralyzed.

JOH 6:47 Verily, verily, I say unto you, He that believeth **on me** hath everlasting life.

I tell you the truth, he who believes has everlasting life.

JOH 11:41 Then they took away the stone **from the place where the dead was laid.**

So they took away the stone.

JOH 17:12 While I was with them **in the world,** I kept them in thy name...

While I was with them, I protected them and kept them safe by that name you gave me...

ACT 10:6 He lodgeth with one Simon a tanner, whose house is by the sea side: **he shall tell thee what thou oughtest to do.**

He is staying with Simon the tanner whose house is by the sea.

ACT 20:32 And now, **brethren,** I commend you to God, and to the word of his grace,...

Now I commit you to God and the word of his grace.

ACT 24:6–8 Who also hath gone about to profane the temple: whom we took, **and would have judged according to our law. But the chief captain Lysias came upon us, and with great violence took him away out of our hands, Commanding his accusers to come unto thee:** by examining of whom thyself mayest take knowledge of all these things, whereof we accuse him.

and even tried to desecrate the temple; so we seized him. By examining him yourself you will be able to learn the truth about all these charges we are bringing against him.

ACT 24:15 And have hope toward God, which they themselves also allow, that there shall be a resurrection **of the dead,** both of the just and unjust.

And I have the same hope in God as these men, that there will be a resurrection of both the righteous and the wicked.

ACT 28:16 And when we came to Rome, **the centurion delivered the prisoners to the captain of the guard:** but Paul was suffered to dwell by himself with a soldier that kept him.

When we got to Rome, Paul was allowed to live by himself, with a soldier to guard him.

ACT 28:29 **And when he had said these words, the Jews departed, and had great reasoning among themselves.**

———

ROM 1:29 Being filled with all unrighteousness, **fornication,** wickedness,…

They have become filled with every kind of wickedness, evil, greed…

ROM 9:28 For he will finish the work, and cut it short in **righteousness: because a short work will the Lord make upon the earth.**

For the Lord will carry out his sentence on earth with speed and finality.

ROM 10:15 And how shall they preach, except they be sent? as it is written, How beautiful are the feet of them that **preach the gospel of peace,** and bring glad tidings of good things!

And how can they preach unless they are sent? As it is written, How beautiful are the feet of those who bring good news.

ROM 13:9 …Thou shalt not steal, **Thou shalt not bear false witness,** thou shalt not covet;…

…"Do not steal," "Do not covet,"…

ROM 14:6 He that regardeth the day, regardeth it unto the Lord; **and he that regardeth not the day, to the Lord he doth not regard it. He that eateth, eateth to the Lord, for he giveth God thanks;** and he that eateth not, to the Lord he eateth not, and giveth God thanks.

He who regards one day as special does so to the Lord, for he gives thanks to God; and he who abstains does so to the Lord and gives thanks to God.

ROM 14:21 It is good neither to eat flesh, nor to drink wine, nor any thing whereby thy brother stumbleth, **or is offended, or is made weak.**

It is better not to eat meat or drink wine or to do anything that will cause your brother to fall.

ROM 15:29 And I am sure that, when I come unto you, I shall come in the fulness of the blessing **of the gospel** of Christ.

I know that when I come to you, I will come in the full measure of the blessing of Christ.

1CO 5:7 Purge out therefore the old leaven, that ye may be a new lump, as ye are unleavened. For even Christ our passover is sacrificed **for us:**

Get rid of the old yeast that you may be a new batch without yeast as you really are. For Christ our Passover lamb, has been sacrificed.

1CO 7:5 ...that ye may give yourselves to **fasting and** prayer; and come together again,

...so that you may devote yourselves to prayer. Then come together again...

1CO 7:39 The wife is bound **by the law** as long as her husband liveth; but if her husband be dead, she is at liberty to be married to whom she will; only in the Lord.

A woman is bound to her husband as long as he lives. But if her husband dies, she is free to marry anyone she wishes, but he must belong to the Lord.

1CO 11:24 And when he had given thanks, he brake it, and said, **Take, eat:** this is my body, which is **broken** for you: this do in remembrance of me.

And when he had given thanks, he broke it and said, "This is my body which is for you: do this in remembrance of me."

GAL 3:1 O foolish Galatians, who hath bewitched you, **that ye should not obey the truth,**...

You foolish Galatians! Who has bewitched you?

EPH 5:30 For we are members of his body, **of his flesh, and of his bones**.

For we are members of his body.

EPH 6:10 Finally, **my brethren,** be strong in the Lord, and in the power of his might.

Finally, be strong in the Lord and in his mighty power.

PHI 3:16 Nevertheless, whereto we have already attained, let us walk **by the same rule, let us mind the same thing**.

Only let us live up to what we have already attained.

COL 1:14 In whom we have redemption **through his blood,** even the forgiveness of sins:

In whom we have redemption, the forgiveness of sins.

COL 3:6 For which things' sake the wrath of God cometh **on the children of disobedience:**

Because of these, the wrath of God is coming.

2TH 1:8 **In flaming fire** taking vengeance on them that know not God,

He will punish those who do not know God.

1TI 1:17 Now unto the King eternal, immortal, invisible, the only **wise** God,

Now to the King eternal, immortal, invisible, the only God,

1TI 4:12 Let no man despise thy youth; but be thou an example of the believers, in word, in conversation, charity, **in spirit,** in faith, purity.

Don't let anyone look down on you because you are young, but set an example for the believers in speech, in life, in love, in faith and in purity.

1TI 6:5 Perverse disputings of men of corrupt minds, and destitute of the truth, supposing that gain is godliness: **from such withdraw thyself.**

And constant friction between men of corrupt mind, who have been robbed of the truth and who think that godliness is a means to financial gain.

2TI 1:11 Whereunto I am appointed a preacher, and an apostle, and a teacher **of the Gentiles.**

And of this gospel I was appointed a herald and an apostle and a teacher.

PHM 1:12 Whom I have sent again: **thou therefore receive him,** that is, mine own bowels:

I am sending him – who is my very heart – back to you.

HEB 1:3 Who being the brightness of his glory, and the express image of his person, and upholding all things by the word of his power, when he had **by himself** purged our sins, sat down on the right hand of the Majesty on high:

The Son is the radiance of God's glory and the exact representation of his being, sustaining all things by his powerful word. After he had provided purification for sins, he sat down at the right hand of the Majesty in heaven.

HEB 2:7 Thou madest him a little lower than the angels; thou crownedst him with glory and honour, **and didst set him over the works of thy hands:**

You made him a little lower than the angels; you crowned him with glory and honor.

HEB 7:21 …The Lord sware and will not repent, Thou art a priest for ever **after the order of Melchisedec.**

…"The Lord has sworn and will not change his mind: You are a priest forever."

HEB 10:34 For ye had compassion of me in my bonds, and took joyfully the spoiling of your goods, knowing in yourselves that ye have **in heaven** a better and an enduring substance.

You sympathized with those in prison and joyfully accepted the confiscation of your property, because you knew that you yourselves had better and lasting possessions.

1PE 4:1 Forasmuch then as Christ hath suffered **for us** in the flesh,

Therefore, since Christ suffered in his body.

1PE 4:14 If ye be reproached for the name of Christ, happy are ye; for the spirit of glory and of God resteth upon you: **on their part he is evil spoken of, but on your part he is glorified.**

If you are insulted because of the name of Christ, you are blessed, for the Spirit of glory and of God rests on you.

1PE 5:11 To him be **glory and** dominion for ever and ever. Amen.

To him be the power for ever and ever. Amen.

2PE 2:17 These are wells without water, clouds that are carried with a tempest; to whom the mist of darkness is reserved **for ever.**

These men are springs without water and mists driven by a storm. Blackest darkness is reserved for them.

1JO 2:7 Brethren, I write no new commandment unto you, but an old commandment which ye had from the beginning. The old commandment is the word which ye have heard **from the beginning.**

Dear friends, I am not writing you a new command but an old one, which you have had since the beginning. This old command is the message you have heard.

JUD 25 To the only **wise** God our Saviour, be glory and majesty, dominion and power, both now and ever. Amen.

To the only God our Savior be glory, majesty, power and authority, through Jesus Christ our Lord, before all ages, now and forevermore! Amen.

REV 2:13 I know **thy works,** and where thou dwellest...

I know where you live...

REV 6:1 And I saw when the Lamb opened one of the seals, and I heard, as it were the noise of thunder, one of the four beasts saying, Come **and see.**
(Also in verses 3, 5, and 7)

I watched as the Lamb opened the first of the seven seals. Then I heard one of the four living creatures say in a voice like thunder, "Come."

REV 11:17 Saying, We give thee thanks, O LORD God Almighty, which art, and wast, **and art to come;** because thou hast taken to thee thy great power, and hast reigned.

saying: We give thanks to you, Lord God Almighty, who is and who was, because you have taken your great power and have begun to reign.

REV 12:12 ...Woe to **the inhabiters of** the earth and of the sea! for the devil is come down unto you,...

..."But woe to the earth and the sea, because the devil has gone down to you!

REV 16:17 And the seventh angel poured out his vial into the air; and there came a great voice out of the temple **of heaven,** from the throne, saying, It is done.

The seventh angel poured out his bowl into the air, and out of the temple came a loud voice from the throne, saying, "It is done."

REV 21:24 And the nations **of them which are saved** shall walk in the light of it: and the kings of the earth do bring their glory and **honour** into it.

The nations will walk by its light, and the kings of the earth will bring their splendor into it.

Remember, none of the boldfaced/underlined words appear in the NIV text (1978 edition). Occasional reference is made to omitted passages in footnotes. Many of the passages which the NIV does include (but are omitted by the other modern versions) are given a footnote expressing doubt.

Section B
Names of Christ and
Titles of Deity Missing

The omission of Sacred Names causes the first doubts over the trustworthiness of the modern translations. Names of Deity are missing, and they are missing frequently! The totals of such omissions in two of the most popular versions – The New American Standard and The New International – are tabulated below. Where these Names are in combination, they have been counted separately.

	N.A.S.V.	N.I.V.
Jesus	73	36
Christ	43	44
Lord	35	35
God	33	31
Other Names	30	30
Total Missing Names	**214**	**176**

King James Bible	New International Version
MAT 6:33 But seek ye first the kingdom **of God,** and his righteousness:...	But seek first his kingdom and his righteousness,...
MAT 8:29 And, behold, they cried out, saying, What have we to do with thee, **Jesus,** thou Son of God?	What do you want with us, Son of God? they shouted.
MAT 13:36 Then **Jesus** sent the multitude away, and went into the house: and his disciples came unto him, saying, Declare unto us the parable of the tares of the field.	Then he left the crowd and went into the house. His disciples came to him and said, "Explain to us the parable of the weeds in the field."
MAT 13:51 Jesus saith unto them, Have ye understood all these things? They say unto him, Yea, **Lord.**	Have you understood all these things? Jesus asked. Yes, they replied.

MAT 15:30   And great multitudes came unto him, having with them those that were lame, blind, dumb, maimed, and many others, and cast them down at **Jesus'** feet; and he healed them:

Great crowds came to him, bringing the lame, the blind, the crippled, the dumb and many others, and laid them at his feet; and he healed them.

MAT 16:20   Then charged he his disciples that they should tell no man that he was **Jesus** the Christ.

Then he warned his disciples not to tell anyone that he was the Christ.

MAT 17:20   And **Jesus** said unto them, Because of your unbelief: for verily I say unto you, If ye have faith as a grain of mustard seed,...

He replied "Because you have so little faith, I tell you the truth, if you have faith as small as a mustard seed...

MAT 18:2   And **Jesus** called a little child unto him, and set him in the midst of them,

He called a little child and had him stand among them.

MAT 18:11   **For the Son of man is come to save that which was lost.**

———

MAT 19:17   And he said unto him, Why callest thou me good? there is none good but one, **that is, God:**

"Why do you ask me about what is good?" Jesus replied, "There is only One who is good."

MAT 21:12   And Jesus went into the temple **of God,** and cast out all them that sold and bought in the temple,...

Jesus entered the temple area and drove out all who were buying and selling there.

MAT 22:30   For in the resurrection they neither marry, nor are given in marriage, but are as the angels of **God** in heaven.

At the resurrection people will neither marry nor be given in marriage; they will be like the angels in heaven.

MAT 22:32   ...**God** is not the God of the dead, but of the living.

...He is not the God of the dead but of the living.

MAT 23:8   But be not ye called Rabbi: for one is your Master, **even Christ;** and all ye are brethren.

"But you are not to be called 'Rabbi', for you have only one Master and you are all brothers."

MAT 24:2 And **Jesus** said unto them, See ye not all these things? Verily I say unto you, There shall not be left here one stone upon another, that shall not be thrown down.

"Do you see all these things?" he asked. "I tell you the truth, not one stone here will be left on another; every one will be thrown down."

MAT 25:13 Watch therefore, for ye know neither the day nor the hour **wherein the Son of man cometh.**

Therefore keep watch, because you do not know the day or the hour.

MAT 28:6 He is not here: for he is risen, as he said. Come, see the place where the **Lord** lay.

He is not here; he has risen, just as he said. Come and see the place where he lay.

MAR 5:13 And **forthwith Jesus** gave them leave. And the unclean spirits went out, and entered into the swine:

He gave them permission, and the evil spirits came out and went into the pigs.

MAR 6:33 And the people saw them departing, and many knew **him,** and afoot thither out of all cities, outwent them, and came together unto **him.**

But many who saw them leaving recognized them and ran on foot from all the towns and got there ahead of them.

MAR 7:27 But **Jesus** said unto her, Let the children first be filled:…

"First let the children eat all they want," he told her,…

MAR 9:24 And straightway the father of the child cried out, **and said with tears, Lord,** I believe; help thou mine unbelief.

Immediately the boy's father exclaimed, "I do believe; help me overcome my unbelief."

MAR 11:10 Blessed be the kingdom of our father David, **that cometh in the name of the Lord:** Hosanna in the highest.

Blessed is the coming kingdom of our father David! Hosanna in the highest!

MAR 11:14 And **Jesus** answered and said unto it, No man eat fruit of thee hereafter for ever.

Then he said to the tree, "May no one ever eat fruit from you again."

MAR 11:26 **But if ye do not forgive, neither will your Father which is in heaven forgive your trespasses.**

———

MAR 12:27 He is not the God of the dead, but the **God** of the living:...

He is not the God of the dead, but of the living.

MAR 14:45 And as soon as he was come, he goeth straightway to him, and saith, Master, **master;** and kissed him.

Going at once to Jesus, Judas said, "Rabbi!" and kissed him.

LUK 2:40 And the child grew, and waxed strong **in spirit,** filled with wisdom: and the grace of God was upon him.

And the child grew and became strong; he was filled with wisdom, and the grace of God was upon him.

LUK 4:4 And Jesus answered him, saying, It is written, That man shall not live by bread alone, **but by every word of God.**

Jesus answered, "It is written: Man does not live on bread alone."

LUK 4:41 And devils also came out of many, crying out, and saying, Thou art **Christ** the Son of God...

Moreover, demons came out of many people, shouting, "You are the Son of God."

LUK 7:22 Then **Jesus** answering said unto them, Go your way, and tell John what things ye have seen and heard;...

So he replied to the messengers "Go back and report to John what you have seen and heard:...

LUK 7:31 **And the Lord said,** Whereunto then shall I liken the men of this generation? and to what are they like?

"To what, then, can I compare the people of this generation? What are they like?

LUK 9:56 **For the Son of man is not come to destroy men's lives, but to save them.** And they went to another village.

and they went to another village.

LUK 9:57 And it came to pass, that, as they went in the way, a certain man said unto him, **Lord,** I will follow thee whithersoever thou goest.

As they were walking along the road, a man said to him, "I will follow you wherever you go."

LUK 12:31 But rather seek ye the kingdom **of God;** and all these things shall be added unto you.

But seek his kingdom, and these things will be given to you as well.

LUK 13:25 When once the master of the house is risen up, and hath shut to the door, and ye begin to stand without, and to knock at the door, saying, **Lord, Lord,** open unto us;

Once the owner of the house gets up and closes the door, you will stand outside knocking and pleading, "Sir, open the door for us."

LUK 21:4 For all these have of their abundance cast in unto the offerings **of God:** but she of her penury hath cast in all the living that she had.

All these people gave their gifts out of their wealth; but she out of her poverty put in all she had to live on.

LUK 22:31 **And the Lord said,** Simon, Simon, behold, Satan hath desired **to have you,** that he may sift you as wheat:

Simon, Simon, Satan has asked to sift you as wheat.

LUK 23:42 And he said unto Jesus, **Lord,** remember me when thou comest into thy kingdom.

Then he said, "Jesus, remember me when you come into your kingdom."

JOH 4:16 **Jesus** saith unto her, Go, call thy husband, and come hither.

He told her, "Go call your husband and come back."

JOH 4:42 ...and know that this is indeed **the Christ,** the Saviour of the world.

...and we know that this man really is the Saviour of the world.

JOH 4:46 So **Jesus** came again into Cana of Galilee,...

Once more he visited Cana in Galilee,...

JOH 5:30 ...because I seek not mine own will, but the will of the **Father** which hath sent me.

...for I seek not to please myself but him who sent me.

JOH 6:39 And this is the **Father's** will which hath sent me,...

And this is the will of him who sent me.

JOH 6:69 And we believe and are sure that thou art that **Christ, the Son** of **the living** God.

We believe and know that you are the Holy One of God.

JOH 8:11 She said, No man, **Lord.** And Jesus said unto her, Neither do I condemn thee: go, and sin no more.

"No one, sir," she said. "Then neither do I condemn you." Jesus declared. "Go now and leave your life of sin."

JOH 8:20 These words spake **Jesus** in the treasury,...

He spoke these words while teaching in the temple area.

JOH 8:29 And he that sent me is with me: the **Father** hath not left me alone; for I do always those things that please him.

"The one who sent me is with me; he has not left me alone, for I always do what pleases him."

JOH 9:35 ...Dost thou believe on the Son of **God?**

...Do you believe in the Son of man?

JOH 16:16 A little while, and ye shall not see me: and again, a little while, and ye shall see me, **because I go to the Father.**

In a little while you will see me no more, and then after a little while you will see me.

JOH 19:38 ...besought Pilate that he might take away the body of Jesus: and Pilate gave him leave. He came therefore, and took the body **of Jesus.**

...asked Pilate for the body of Jesus...with Pilate's permission, he came and took the body.

ACT 2:30 Therefore being a prophet, and knowing that God had sworn with an oath to him, that of the fruit of his loins, **according to the flesh, he would raise up Christ** to sit on his throne;

But he was a prophet and knew that God had promised him an oath that he would place one of his descendants on his throne.

ACT 3:26 Unto you first God, having raised up his **Son Jesus,** sent him to bless you, in turning away every one of you from his iniquities.

"When God raised up his servant he sent him first to you to bless you by turning each of you from your wicked ways."

ACT 4:24 ...Lord, **thou art God,** which made heaven, and earth...

..."Sovereign Lord," they said, "you made the heaven and the earth..."

ACT 7:30 And when forty years were expired, there appeared to him in the wilderness of mount Sina an angel **of the Lord** in a flame of fire in a bush.

After forty years had passed, an angel appeared to Moses in the flames of a burning bush in the desert near Mount Sinai.

ACT 7:32 Saying, I am the God of thy fathers, the God of Abraham, and the **God** of Isaac, and the **God** of Jacob.

'I am the God of your fathers, the God of Abraham, Isaac and Jacob.'

ACT 7:37 ...A prophet shall **the Lord** your God raise up unto you of your brethren, like unto me; **him shall ye hear.**

...'God will send you a prophet like me from your own people.'

ACT 8:37 **And Philip said, If thou believest with all thine heart, thou mayest. And he answered and said, I believe that Jesus Christ is the Son of God.**

———

ACT 9:5-6 And he said, Who art thou, Lord? And **the Lord** said, I am Jesus whom thou persecutest: **it is hard for thee to kick against the pricks. And he trembling and astonished said, Lord, what wilt thou have me to do? And the Lord said** unto him, Arise, and go into the city, and it shall be told thee what thou must do.

"Who are you, Lord?" Saul asked. "I am Jesus, whom you are persecuting," he replied. "Now get up and go into the city, and you will be told what you must do."

ACT 9:29 **And he spake boldly in the name of the Lord Jesus,** and disputed against the Grecians:

He talked and debated with the Grecian Jews,...

ACT 15:11 But we believe that through the grace of the LORD Jesus **Christ** we shall be saved, even as they.

No! We believe it is through the grace of our Lord Jesus that we are saved, just as they are."

ACT 15:18 **Known unto God are all his works** from the beginning of the world.

that have been known for ages.

ACT 16:31 And they said, Believe on the Lord Jesus **Christ,** and thou shalt be saved, and thy house.

They replied, "Believe in the Lord Jesus, and you will be saved—you and your household."

ACT 19:4 …that they should believe on him which should come after him, that is, on **Christ** Jesus.

"…to believe in the one coming after him, that is, in Jesus."

ACT 19:10 …so that all they which dwelt in Asia heard the word of the Lord **Jesus,** both Jews and Greeks.

…so that all the Jews and Greeks who lived in the province of Asia heard the word of the Lord.

ACT 20:21 Testifying both to the Jews, and also to the Greeks, repentance toward God, and faith toward our Lord Jesus **Christ.**

I have declared to both Jews and Greeks that they must turn to God in repentance and have faith in our Lord Jesus.

ACT 20:25 And now, behold, I know that ye all, among whom I have gone preaching the kingdom **of God,** shall see my face no more.

Now I know that none of you among whom I have gone about preaching the kingdom will ever see me again.

ACT 22:16 And now why tarriest thou? arise, and be baptized, and wash away thy sins, calling on the name of the **Lord.**

And now what are you waiting for? Get up, be baptised and wash your sins away, calling on his name.

ACT 23:9 …We find no evil in this man: but if a spirit or an angel hath spoken to him, **let us not fight against God.**

…We find nothing wrong with this man, they said. What if a spirit or an angel has spoken to him?

ROM 1:16 For I am not ashamed of the gospel **of Christ:** for it is the power of God unto salvation to every one that believeth; to the Jew first, and also to the Greek.

I am not ashamed of the gospel, because it is the power of God for the salvation of everyone who believes: first for the Jew, then for the Gentile.

ROM 6:11 Likewise reckon ye also yourselves to be dead indeed unto sin, but alive unto God through Jesus Christ **our Lord.**

In the same way, count yourselves dead to sin but alive to God in Christ Jesus.

ROM 8:1 There is therefore now no condemnation to them which are in Christ Jesus, **who walk not after the flesh, but after the Spirit.**

Therefore, there is now no condemnation for those who are in Christ Jesus.

ROM 14:6 He that regardeth the day, regardeth it unto the Lord; **and he that regardeth not the day, to the Lord he doth not regard it. He that eateth, eateth to the Lord,** for he giveth God thanks; and he that eateth not, to the Lord he eateth not, and giveth God thanks.

He who regards one day as special, does so to the Lord, for he gives thanks to God; and he who abstains does so to the Lord and gives thanks to God.

ROM 15:8   Now I say that **Jesus** Christ was a minister of the circumcision for the truth of God,...

For I tell you that Christ has become a servant of the Jews on behalf of God's truth.

ROM 15:19   Through mighty signs and wonders, by the power of the Spirit **of God;**...

by the power of signs and miracles, through the power of the Spirit.

ROM 16:18   For they that are such serve not our Lord **Jesus** Christ, but their own belly; and by good words and fair speeches deceive the hearts of the simple.

For such people are not serving our Lord Christ, but their own appetites. By smooth talk and flattery they deceive the minds naive people.

ROM 16:24   **The grace of our Lord Jesus Christ be with you all. Amen.**

———

1CO 1:14 I thank **God** that I baptized none of you, but Crispus and Gaius;

I am thankful that I did not baptize any of you except Crispus and Gaius.

1CO 5:4   In the name of our Lord Jesus **Christ,** when ye are gathered together, and my spirit, with the power of our Lord Jesus **Christ.**

When you are assembled in the name of our Lord Jesus and I am with you in spirit, and the power of our Lord Jesus is present,

1CO 5:5 To deliver such an one unto Satan for the destruction of the flesh, that the spirit may be saved in the day of the Lord **Jesus.**

hand this man over to Satan, so that the sinful nature may be destroyed and his spirit saved on the day of the Lord.

1CO 6:20 For ye are bought with a price: therefore glorify God in your body, **and in your spirit, which are God's.**

You were bought at a price. Therefore honour God with your body.

1CO 9:1 Am I not an apostle? am I not free? have I not seen Jesus **Christ** our Lord? are not ye my work in the Lord?

Am I not free? Am I not an apostle? Have I not seen Jesus our Lord? Are you not the result of my work in the Lord?

1CO 9:18 What is my reward then? Verily that, when I preach the gospel, I may make the gospel **of Christ** without charge,...

What then is my reward? Just this: that in preaching the gospel I may offer it free of charge.

1CO 10:28 But if any man say unto you, This is offered in sacrifice unto idols, eat not for his sake that shewed it, and for conscience sake: **for the earth is the Lord's, and the fulness thereof:**

But if anyone says to you, "This has been offered in sacrifice." then do not eat it, both for the sake of the man who told you and for conscience sake.

1CO 15:47 The first man is of the earth, earthy; the second man is **the Lord** from heaven.

The first man was of the dust of the earth, the second man from heaven.

1CO 16:22 If any man love not the Lord **Jesus Christ,** let him be Anathema Maranatha.

If anyone does not love the Lord—a curse be on him. Come, O Lord!

1CO 16:23 The grace of **our** Lord Jesus **Christ** be with you.

The grace of the Lord Jesus be with you.

2CO 4:6 For God, who commanded the light to shine out of darkness, hath shined in our hearts, to give the light of the knowledge of the glory of God in the face of **Jesus** Christ.

For God, who said, "Let light shine out of darkness," made his light shine in our hearts to give us the light of the knowledge of the glory of God in the face of Christ.

2CO 4:10 Always bearing about in the body the dying of **the Lord** Jesus, that the life also of Jesus might be made manifest in our body.

We always carry around in our body the death of Jesus, so that the life of Jesus may also be revealed in our body.

2CO 5:18 And all things are of God, who hath reconciled us to himself by **Jesus** Christ and hath given to us the ministry of reconciliation.

All this is from God, who reconciled us to himself, through Christ and gave us the ministry of reconciliation.

2CO 10:7 Do ye look on things after the outward appearance? If any man trust to himself that he is Christ's, let him of himself think this again, that, as he is **Christ's,** even so are we Christ's.

You are looking only on the surface of things. If anyone is confident that he belongs to Christ, he should consider again that we belong to Christ just as much as he.

2CO 11:31 The God and Father of **our** Lord Jesus **Christ,** which is blessed for evermore, knoweth that I lie not.

The God and Father of the Lord Jesus, who is to be praised forever, knows that I am not lying.

GAL 3:17 And this I say, that the covenant, that was confirmed before of God **in Christ,**...

What I mean is this: the law, introduced 430 years later, does not set aside the covenant previously established by God...

GAL 4:7 Wherefore thou art no more a servant, but a son; and if a son, then an heir of God **through Christ.**

So you are no longer a slave, but a son; and since you are a son, God has made you also an heir.

GAL 6:15 For **in Christ Jesus** neither circumcision availeth any thing, nor uncircumcision, but a new creature.

Neither circumcision nor uncircumcision means anything; what counts is a new creation.

GAL 6:17 From henceforth let no man trouble me: for I bear in my body the marks of **the Lord** Jesus.

Finally, let no one cause me trouble, for I bear on my body the marks of Jesus.

EPH 3:9 And to make all men see what is the fellowship of the mystery, which from the beginning of the world hath been hid in God, who created all things **by Jesus Christ:**

And to make plain to everyone the administration of this mystery, which for ages past was kept hidden in God, who created all things.

EPH 3:14 For this cause I bow my knees unto the Father **of our Lord Jesus Christ.**

For this reason I kneel before the Father.

EPH 5:9 (For the fruit of the **Spirit** is in all goodness and righteousness and truth;)

(for the fruit of the light consists in all goodness, righteousness and truth)

PHI 4:13 I can do all things through **Christ** which strengtheneth me.

I can do everything through him who gives me strength.

COL 1:2 ...Grace be unto you, and peace, from God our Father **and the Lord Jesus Christ.**

...Grace and peace to you from God our Father.

COL 1:28 Whom we preach, warning every man, and teaching every man in all wisdom; that we may present every man perfect in Christ **Jesus.**

We proclaim him, admonishing and teaching everyone with all wisdom, so that we may present everyone perfect in Christ.

COL 2:2 ...to the acknowledgment of the mystery of God, **and of the Father,** and of Christ.

...that they may know the mystery of God, namely, Christ,

1TH 1:1 Paul, and Silvanus, and Timotheus, unto the church of the Thessalonians which in God the Father and in the Lord Jesus Christ: Grace and peace **from God the Father, and the Lord Jesus Christ.**

Paul, Silas and Timothy, To the church of the Thessalonians in God our Father and the Lord Jesus Christ: Grace and peace to you.

1TH 2:19 For what is our hope or joy, or crown of rejoicing? Are not even ye in the presence of our Lord Jesus **Christ** as his coming.

For what is our hope, our joy, or our crown in which we will glory in the presence of our Lord Jesus when he comes? Is it not you?

1TH 3:11 Now God himself and our Father, and our Lord Jesus **Christ,** direct our way unto you.

Now may our God and Father himself and our Lord Jesus clear the way for us to come to you.

1TH 3:13 To the end he may stablish your hearts unblameable in holiness before God, even our Father, at the coming of our Lord Jesus **Christ** with all his saints.

May he strengthen your hearts so that you will be blameless and holy in the presence of our God and Father when our Lord Jesus comes with all his holy ones.

2TH 1:8 **In flaming fire** taking vengeance on them that know not God, and that obey not the gospel of our Lord Jesus **Christ:**

He will punish those who do not know God and do not obey the gospel of our Lord Jesus.

2TH 1:12 That the name of our Lord Jesus **Christ** may be glorified in you, and ye in him, according to the grace of our God and the Lord Jesus Christ.

…that the name of our Lord Jesus may be glorified in you, and you in him, according to the grace of our God and the Lord Jesus Christ.

2TH 2:4 Who opposeth and exalteth himself above all that is called God, or that is worshipped; so that he **as God** sitteth in the temple of God, shewing himself that he is God.

He opposes and exalts himself over everything that is called God or is worshiped, and even sets himself up on God's temple, proclaiming himself to be God.

1TI 1:1 Paul, an apostle of Jesus Christ by the commandment of God our Saviour, and **Lord** Jesus Christ, which is our hope;

Paul, an apostle of Christ Jesus by the commandment of God our Savior and of Christ Jesus our hope,

1TI 2:7 Whereunto I am ordained a preacher, and an apostle, (I speak the truth **in Christ,** and lie not;) a teacher of the Gentiles in faith and verity.

And for this purpose I was appointed a herald and an apostle—I am telling the truth, I am not lying—and a teacher of the true faith to the Gentiles.

1TI 3:16 And without controversy great is the mystery of godliness: **God** was manifest in the flesh,…

Beyond all question, the mystery of godliness is great: He appeared in a body,…

1TI 5:21 I charge thee before God, and the **Lord** Jesus Christ, and the elect angels,…

I charge you, in the sight of God and Christ Jesus and the elect angels,…

2TI 4:1 I charge thee therefore before God, and **the Lord** Jesus Christ, who shall judge the quick and the dead at his appearing and his kingdom;

In the presence of God and of Christ Jesus, who will judge the living and the dead, and in view of his appearing and his kingdom, I give you this charge:

2TI 4:22 The Lord **Jesus Christ** be with thy spirit. Grace be with you. Amen.

The Lord be with your spirit. Grace be with you.

TIT 1:4 To Titus, mine own son after the common faith: Grace, mercy, and peace, from God the Father and the **Lord** Jesus Christ our Saviour.

To Titus, my true son in our common faith: Grace and peace from God the Father and Christ Jesus our Saviour.

PHM 1:6 That the communication of thy faith may become effectual by the acknowledging of every good thing which is in you in Christ **Jesus.**

HEB 3:1 Wherefore, holy brethren, partakers of the heavenly calling, consider the Apostle and High Priest of our profession, **Christ** Jesus;

HEB 10:9 Then said he, Lo, I come to do thy will, **O God.** He taketh away the first, that he may establish the second.

HEB 10:30 For we know him that hath said, Vengeance belongeth unto me, I will recompense, **saith the Lord.** And again, The Lord shall judge his people.

1PE 1:22 Seeing ye have purified your souls in obeying the truth **through the Spirit** unto un-feigned love of the brethren, see that ye love one another with a pure heart fervently:

1PE 5:10 But the God of all grace, who hath called us unto his eternal glory by Christ **Jesus,** after that ye have suffered a while, make you perfect, stablish, strengthen, settle you.

1PE 5:14 Greet ye one another with a kiss of charity. Peace be with you all that are in Christ **Jesus. Amen.**

1JO 1:7 But if we walk in the light, as he is in the light, we have fellowship one with another, and the blood of Jesus **Christ** his Son cleanseth us from all sin.

I pray that you may be active in sharing your faith, so that you will have a full understanding of every good thing we have in Christ.

Therefore, holy brothers, who share in the heavenly calling, fix your thoughts on Jesus, the apostle and high priest whom we confess.

Then he said, "Here I am, I have come to do your will." He sets aside the first to establish the second.

For we know him who said, "It is mine to avenge; I will repay," and again, "The Lord will judge his people."

Now that you have purified yourselves by obeying the truth so that you have sincere love for your brothers, love one another deeply, from the heart.

And the God of all grace, who called you to his eternal glory in Christ, after you have suffered a little while, will himself restore you and make you strong, firm and steadfast.

Greet one another with a kiss of love. Peace to all of you who are in Christ.

But if we walk in the light, as he is in the light, we have fellowship with one another, and the blood of Jesus, his Son, purifies us from all sin.

1JO 3:16 Hereby perceive we the love **of God,** because he laid down his life for us: and we ought to lay down our lives for the brethren.

This is how we know what love is: Jesus Christ laid down his life for us. And we ought to lay down our lives for our brothers.

1JO 4:3 And every spirit that confesseth not that Jesus **Christ is come in the flesh** is not of God:...

But every spirit that does not acknowledge Jesus is not from God...

1JO 5:7-8 For there are three that bear record **in heaven, the Father, the Word, and the Holy Ghost: and these three are one. And there are three that bear witness in earth,** the Spirit, and the water, and the blood: and these three agree in one.

For there are three that testify: the Spirit, the water and the blood; and the three are in agreement.

1JO 5:13 These things have I written unto you that believe on the name of the Son of God; that ye may know that ye have eternal life, **and that ye may believe on the name of the Son of God.**

I write these things to you who believe in the name of the Son of God so that you may know that you have eternal life.

2JO 3 Grace be with you, mercy, and peace, from God the Father, and from the **Lord** Jesus Christ, the Son of the Father, in truth and love.

Grace, mercy and peace from God the Father and from Jesus Christ, the Father's Son, will be with us in truth and love.

2JO 9 Whosoever transgresseth, and abideth not in the doctrine of Christ, hath not God. He that abideth in the doctrine **of Christ,** he hath both the Father and the Son.

Anyone who runs ahead and does not continue in the teaching of Christ does not have God; whoever continues in the teaching has both the Father and the Son.

JUD 4 ...ungodly men, turning the grace of our God into lasciviousness, and denying the only Lord God, and our **Lord** Jesus Christ.

...godless men, who change the grace of our God into a license for immorality and deny Jesus Christ our only Sovereign and Lord.

REV 1:8 I am Alpha and Omega, **the beginning and the ending,** saith the Lord, which is, and which was, and which is to come, the Almighty.

"I am the Alpha and the Omega," says the Lord God, "who is, and who was, and who is to come, the Almighty."

REV 1:9 I John, who also am your brother, and companion in tribulation, and in the kingdom and patience of Jesus **Christ,** was in the isle that is called Patmos, for the word of God, and for the testimony of Jesus **Christ.**

I, John, your brother and companion in the suffering and kingdom and patient endurance that are ours in Jesus, was on the island of Patmos because of the word of God and the testimony of Jesus.

REV 1:11 Saying, **I am Alpha and Omega, the first and the last:** and, What thou seest, write in a book, and send it unto the seven churches **which are in Asia;** unto Ephesus, and unto Smyrna, and unto Pergamos,...

which said: "Write on a scroll what you see and send it to the seven churches: to Ephesus, Smyrna, Pergamum, Thyatira, Sardis, Philadelphia and Laodicea."

REV 5:14 And the four beasts said, Amen. And **the four and twenty** elders fell down and worshipped **him that liveth for ever and ever.**

The four living creatures said, "Amen," and the elders fell down and worshiped.

REV 14:5 And in their mouth was found no guile: for they are without fault **before the throne of God.**

No lie was found in their mouths; they are blameless.

REV 16:5 And I heard the angel of the waters say, Thou art righteous, **O Lord,** which art, and wast, and shalt be, because thou hast judged thus.

Then I heard the angel in charge of the waters say: "You are just in these judgments, you who are and who were, the Holy One, because you have so judged;

REV 19:1 And after these things I heard a great voice of much people in heaven, saying, Alleluia; Salvation, and glory, and honour, and power, unto **the Lord** our God:

After this I heard what sounded like the roar of a great multitude in heaven shouting: "Hallelujah! Salvation and glory and power belong to our God,

REV 20:9 And they went up on the breadth of the earth, and compassed the camp of the saints about, and the beloved city: and fire came down from **God out** of heaven, and devoured them.

They marched across the breadth of the earth and surrounded the camp of God's people, the city he loves. But fire came down from heaven and devoured them.

REV 20:12 And I saw the dead, small and great, stand before **God;** and the books were opened: ...

And I saw the dead, great and small, standing before the throne, and books were opened.

REV 21:4 And **God** shall wipe away all tears from their eyes;...

He will wipe every tear from their eyes.

REV 22:21   The grace of our Lord Jesus **Christ** be with you all. Amen.

The grace of the Lord Jesus be with God's people. Amen.

Defenders of the modern versions have sought to minimize the fact of these missing Names of Deity. A typical example is that which the President of the well known Grace Theological Seminary offers in his tract "The King James Only?":

> "One common objection... is that in a
> **relatively few cases** the names 'Christ' and
> 'Lord' are omitted when referring to Jesus."

The previous inventory of hard evidence demonstrates that these Names are missing in much more than "a relatively few cases"!

And it is easier for heaven and earth to pass,

than one tittle of the law to fail.

Luke 16:17

Section C
More Missing Passages

Very few Christians are aware as to how much is actually missing in the modern Bible translations. With the addition of this third list, the full extent of the problem can begin to be realized. The underlined portions are omitted in the New International Version as well as most other twentieth century English versions, and they are also missing in the newer foreign translations.

MAT 5:22   ...whosoever is angry with his brother **without a cause** shall be in danger...

MAT 5:27   Ye have heard that it was said **by them of old time,** Thou shalt not commit adultery:

MAT 6:4   ...and thy Father which seeth in secret himself shall reward thee **openly.**

MAT 6:6   ...thy Father which seeth in secret shall reward thee **openly.**

MAT 6:18   ...and thy Father, which seeth in secret, shall reward thee **openly.**

MAT 15:6   And honour not his father **or his mother,**

MAT 19:16   **Good** Master, what good thing shall I do,...

MAT 19:20   ...All these things have I kept **from my youth up:**

MAT 20:23   ...Ye shall drink indeed of my cup, **and be baptized with the baptism that I am baptized with:**

MAT 20:34   ...and immediately **their eyes** received sight,...

MAT 22:7   But when the king **heard** thereof, he was wroth:...

MAT 22:13   ...Bind him hand and foot, **and take him away,** and cast him into outer darkness, there shall be...

MAT 23:4   For they bind heavy burdens **and grievous to be borne,**...

MAT 23:19   Ye **fools and** blind: for whether is greater,

MAT 24:7	...and there shall be famines, **and pestilences,** and earthquakes,...
MAT 24:48	...that evil servant shall say in his heart, My lord delayeth **his coming;**
MAT 25:31	When the Son of man shall come in his glory, and all the **holy** angels with him,...
MAT 26:3	Then assembled together the chief priests, **and the scribes,** and the elders...
MAT 26:28	For this is my blood of the **new** testament, which is shed...
MAT 26:59	Now the chief priests, **and elders,** and all the council,
MAT 26:60	But found none: yea, though many false witnesses came, **yet found they none.**
MAT 27:42	...**If** he be the King of Israel, let him now come down from the cross,...
MAT 27:64	...lest his disciples come **by night,** and steal him away,...
MAR 1:42	And **as soon as he had spoken,** immediately the leprosy departed...
MAR 2:16	...they said unto his disciples, **How is it** that he eateth and drinketh with publicans and sinners?
MAR 2:22	...else the new wine doth burst the bottles, and the wine **is spilled,**...
MAR 3:15	And to have power **to heal sicknesses,** and to cast out devils:
MAR 4:11	...Unto you it is given **to know** the mystery of the kingdom of God:...
MAR 6:36	...and buy themselves bread: **for they have nothing to eat.**
MAR 7:2	...that is to say, with unwashen, hands, **they found fault.**
MAR 8:9	And they **that had eaten** were about four thousand:...
MAR 8:26	...Neither go into the town, **nor tell it to any in the town.**
MAR 9:29	... This kind can come forth by nothing, but by prayer **and fasting.**
MAR 9:45	...than having two feet to be cast into hell, **into the fire that never shall be quenched:**

MAR 9:49   For every one shall be salted with fire, **and every sacrifice shall be salted with salt.**

MAR 10:21   …and come, **take up the cross,** and follow me.

MAR 11:8   … and others cut down branches off the trees, and strawed them **in the way.**

MAR 11:23   …those things which he saith shall come to pass; he shall have **whatsoever he saith.**

MAR 12:4   …at him **they cast stones,** and wounded him in the head, and **sent him** away shamefully handled.

MAR 12:23   In the resurrection **therefore, when they shall rise,** whose wife shall she be of them?…

MAR 12:29   …The first of **all the commandments** is, Hear, O Israel;…

MAR 12:30   …and with all thy strength: **this is the first commandment.**

MAR 12:33   …and with all the understanding, **and with all the soul,**…

MAR 13:8   …and there shall be famines **and troubles:**…

MAR 13:11   …take no thought beforehand what ye shall speak, **neither do ye premeditate:**…

MAR 14:19   …and to say unto him one by one, Is it I? **and another said, Is it I?**

MAR 14:22   …Take, **eat:** this is my body.

MAR 14:24   …This is my blood of the **new** testament, which is shed for many.

MAR 14:27   …All ye shall be offended **because of me this night:**…

MAR 14:51   …and **the young men** laid hold on him:

MAR 14:70   …thou art a Galilaean, **and thy speech agreeth thereto.**

MAR 15:3   …accused him of many things: **but he answered nothing.**

MAR 15:39   …saw that **he so cried out,** and gave up the ghost,…

LUK 1:29   And **when she saw him,** she was troubled at his saying,…

LUK 2:42   …they went **up to Jerusalem** after the custom of the feast.

LUK 4:18   …he hath sent me **to heal the brokenhearted,** to preach deliverance…

LUK 5:38	But new wine must be put into new bottles; **and both are preserved.**
LUK 7:28	…there is not a greater **prophet** than John the Baptist:
LUK 8:43	…having an issue of blood twelve years, which **had spent all her living upon physicians,**…
LUK 8:45	…When all denied, Peter **and they that were with him** said, Master, the multitude throng thee and press thee, **and sayest thou, Who touched me?**
LUK 8:48	…**be of good comfort:** thy faith hath made thee whole; go in peace.
LUK 8:54	And he **put them all out,** and took her by the hand,…
LUK 9:10	…and went aside privately into **a desert place** belonging to the city…
LUK 11:11	If a son shall ask **bread of any of you** that is a father, **will he give him a stone?** or if he ask a fish,…
LUK 11:44	Woe unto you, **scribes and Pharisees, hypocrites!**…
LUK 11:54	…seeking to catch something out of his mouth, **that they might accuse him.**
LUK 12:39	…had known what hour the thief would come, **he would have watched, and** not have suffered…
LUK 17:3	…If thy brother trespass **against thee,** rebuke him;…
LUK 17:9	…that were commanded **him? I trow not.**
LUK 18:24	And when Jesus saw **that he was very sorrowful,** he said,…
LUK 19:45	…and began to cast out them that sold **therein, and them that bought;**
LUK 20:13	…it may be they will reverence him **when they see him.**
LUK 20:23	But he perceived their craftiness, and said unto them, **Why tempt ye me?**
LUK 20:30	And the second **took her to wife, and he died childless.**
LUK 22:68	… ye will not answer **me, nor let me go.**
LUK 23:23	…And the voices of them **and of the chief priests** prevailed.

LUK 24:1	...spices which they had prepared, **and certain others with them.**
LUK 24:46	...Thus it is written, **and thus it behoved** Christ to suffer,
JOH 1:51	...**Hereafter** ye shall see heaven open,
JOH 3:15	...**should not perish,** but have eternal life.
JOH 5:16	...therefore did the Jews persecute Jesus, **and sought to slay him.**
JOH 6:11	...he distributed **to the disciples, and the disciples** to them...
JOH 6:22	...save **that one whereinto his disciples** were entered,...
JOH 6:65	...except it were given unto him of **my** Father.
JOH 8:9	...**being convicted by their own conscience,** went out one by one, beginning at the eldest, **even unto the last:**...
JOH 8:10	When Jesus had lifted up himself, **and saw none but the woman,** he said unto her, Woman, where are **those thine accusers?**...
JOH 8:28	...but as **my** Father hath taught me,...
JOH 8:38	I speak that which I have seen with **my** Father:...
JOH 8:59	...and went out of the temple, **going through the midst of them, and so passed by.**
JOH 9:6	...and he anointed the eyes of the **blind** man with the clay...
JOH 10:26	...because ye are not of my sheep, **as I said unto you.**
JOH 12:1	...where Lazarus was, **which had been dead,**...
JOH 14:28	...I go unto the Father: for **my** Father is greater than I.
JOH 16:10	...because I go to **my** Father,...
JOH 17:17	Sanctify them through **thy** truth:...
JOH 18:40	Then cried they **all** again, saying,...
JOH 19:16	...And they took Jesus, **and led him away.**
JOH 20:17	...for I am not yet ascended to **my** Father:...
ACT 3:11	And as **the lame man which was healed** held Peter and John,

ACT 5:16	There came also a multitude out of the cities round about **unto** Jerusalem,...
ACT 6:13	...ceaseth not to speak **blasphemous** words against this holy place,...
ACT 7:37	...A prophet shall the Lord your God raise up unto you of your brethren, like unto me; **him shall ye hear.**
ACT 10:12	Wherein were all manner of fourfooted beasts of the earth, **and wild beasts,**...
ACT 10:21	Then Peter went down to the men **which were sent unto him from Cornelius;**...
ACT 10:30	...Four days ago I was **fasting** until this hour;...
ACT 10:32	...he is lodged in the house of one Simon a tanner by the sea side: **who, when he cometh, shall speak unto thee.**
ACT 13:45	...spake against those things which were spoken by Paul, **contradicting and blaspheming.**
ACT 15:23	And they wrote letters by them **after this manner;**...
ACT 15:24	...subverting your souls, saying, **Ye must be circumcised, and keep the law:**...
ACT 17:5	But the Jews **which believed not,** moved with envy, took unto them...
ACT 17:26	And hath made of one **blood** all nations of men...
ACT 18:17	Then all **the Greeks** took Sosthenes,...
ACT 18:21	But bade them farewell, saying, **I must by all means keep this feast that cometh in Jerusalem:**...
ACT 20:15	...we arrived at Samos, **and tarried at Trogyllium;**...
ACT 21:8	And the next day we **that were of Paul's company** departed,...
ACT 21:22	What is it therefore? **the multitude must needs come together: for** they will hear...
ACT 21:25	...and concluded **that they observe no such thing,** save only that they keep themselves from...
ACT 22:9	And they that were with me saw indeed the light, **and were afraid;**...

ACT 22:20	...I also was standing by, and consenting **unto his death,**...
ACT 22:26	...and told the chief captain, saying, **Take heed** what thou doest:...
ACT 23:12	And when it was day, **certain of** the Jews banded together,...
ACT 23:15	...that he bring him down unto you **to morrow,**...
ACT 24:26	He hoped also that money should have been given him of Paul, **that he might loose him:**...
ACT 25:16	...to deliver any man **to die,** before that he which is accused...
ACT 26:30	**And when he had thus spoken,** the king rose up,...
ACT 28:16	And when we came to Rome, **the centurion delivered the prisoners to the captain of the guard:**...
ROM 9:32	...they sought it not by faith, but as it were by the works **of the law**...
ROM 11:6	And if by grace, then is it no more of works: otherwise grace is no more grace. **But if it be of works, then it is no more grace: otherwise work is no more work.**
ROM 15:24	Whensoever I take my journey into Spain, **I will come to you:**
ROM 15:29	...I shall come in the fulness of the blessing **of the gospel** of Christ.
1CO 6:20	...glorify God in your body, **and in your spirit, which are God's.**
1CO 7:39	The wife is bound **by the law** as long as her husband liveth;
1CO 9:22	To the weak became I **as** weak,...
1CO 10:28	...and for conscience sake: **for the earth is the Lord's, and the fulness thereof:**
2CO 5:17	...old things are passed away; behold, **all things** are become new.
GAL 5:19	...**Adultery,** fornication, uncleanness, lasciviousness,
GAL 5:21	Envyings, **murders,** drunkenness,...
EPH 4:9	...that he also descended **first** into the lower parts of the earth?
EPH 4:17	...that ye henceforth walk not as **other** Gentiles walk,...

COL 2:18	...intruding into those things which he hath **not** seen,...
1TH 2:15	Who both killed the Lord Jesus, and **their own** prophets,...
1TI 5:4	...for that is **good and** acceptable before God.
1TI 5:16	If any **man or** woman that believeth have widows,...
1TI 6:7	For we brought nothing into this world, and **it is certain** we can carry nothing out.
TIT 1:4	...Grace, **mercy,** and peace, from God the Father...
HEB 2:7	...thou crownedst him with glory and honour, **and didst set him over the works of thy hands:**
HEB 3:6	...if we hold fast the confidence and the rejoicing of the hope **firm unto the end.**
HEB 8:12	...and their sins **and their iniquities** will I remember no more.
HEB 10:34	...that ye have **in heaven** a better and an enduring substance.
HEB 11:11	...received strength to conceive seed, and was **delivered of a child** when she was past age,...
HEB 11:13	...but having seen them afar off, **and were persuaded of them,**...
HEB 12:20	...if so much as a beast touch the mountain, it shall be stoned, **or thrust through with a dart:**
HEB 13:21	Make you perfect in every good **work** to do his will,...
JAM 4:4	Ye **adulterers** and adulteresses, know ye not...
JAM 5:5	...ye have nourished your hearts, **as** in a day of slaughter.
1PE 3:16	...whereas they speak evil of you, **as of evildoers,**...
1PE 4:3	For the time past **of our life** may suffice us...
1PE 5:5	...Yea, all of you **be subject** one to another,...
2PE 3:10	But the day of the Lord will come as a thief **in the night;**
REV 2:3	...for my name's sake **hast laboured,** and hast not fainted.
REV 2:9	I know thy **works, and** tribulation,...
REV 2:13	I know **thy works, and** where thou dwellest,...
REV 2:20	Notwithstanding I have a **few things** against thee...

REV 5:4   ...no man was found worthy to open **and to read** the book,...

REV 11:1   ...**and the angel stood,** saying, Rise, and measure the temple...

REV 13:10   He that **leadeth** into captivity shall go into captivity:...

REV 15:2   ...gotten the victory over the beast, and over his image, and **over his mark,**...

REV 16:17   ...and there came a great voice out of the temple **of heaven,**

REV 19:1   ...Alleluia; Salvation, and glory, **and honour,** and power, unto the Lord...

O diligent and patient Christian reader, can you not perceive – do you not discern that the sections which have been underlined in these first three presentations are in fact the very Words of the Living God?

The evidence is clearly before you. No Hebrew or Greek scholar need be consulted. Lexicon, commentary, seminary professor, text critic etc. need not be sought out for the truth. Does not the Spirit of God bear witness to your spirit that these passages are Holy Scripture?

Neither should the reader be lulled into thinking that the contents of this manuscript is anywhere near a complete documentation of the numerous omissions and other alterations to be found in the NIV (as well as the other modern translations). Indeed, that which you have before you in this book is merely a superficial sampling.

The issue before us is paramount. As there are only two distinct types of Greek texts, the *Aleph*/B[1] and the *Textus Receptus*[2], if the underscored

---

[1] *Vaticanus* B and *Sinaiticus Aleph* (א) are the Greek manuscript foundation from which the Westcott-Hort, Nestle, and UBS "critical" Greek texts are derived. For all practical purposes, they are synonymous terms. They are the Greek texts from which the modern translations are derived.

[2] The *Textus Receptus* (Received Text) is the Greek foundation from which the King James (and nearly all English translations that preceded it during the century before its 1611 production, e.g., The Great Bible, Bishop's, Matthew's, Geneva, etc.) are derived. Other similar and/or synonymous entities are the "Traditional Text", Byzantine, Syrian, and "majority text".

portions are Scripture then the *Aleph*/B text and all translations derived from it must been seen as false and rejected.

If these omitted words are Scripture, then the *Textus Receptus* must be seen as the Biblical Greek text and the King James Bible must then be viewed as the faithful English rendering of that text. A decision must be made – and yet there is more.

Section D
Hell Diminished or Missing

The doctrine of eternal hell is a fearful Bible truth. The word itself has, from the beginnings of the English language, always had a fixed and established meaning. "The wicked shall be turned into hell and all the nations that forget God" (Psalms 9:17) is very plain. In fact, for many (including preachers and Bible translators) it is apparently too plain. Many people today do not mind using the word in their daily conversation but do not like seeing it in the Bible.

Modern translations have tried to make the Bible more palatable and socially acceptable by taking some of the terror out of the fact that a man or woman who dies outside of faith in Jesus Christ goes to an eternal and conscious hell.

Translators do this in two ways. First, the word is often left in its un-translated Hebrew or Greek form (Sheol or Hades), thus greatly diminishing its impact upon an English reader. The New American Standard Version frequently reverts to this practice. Yet in Greek mythology Hades is merely the home of the dead beneath the earth – not a place of judgment and eternal punishment. Secondly, some simply translate sheol as "death" or "grave". The Jehovah's Witness "Bible" does this, and (if you can believe it!) the New International Version is guilty of the same stratagem.

In the previous lists, the point at issue has been the underlying Greek text of the New Testament. Nearly all modern versions are founded on a radically different text from the King James Bible (KJB). This is the reason for the many omissions which we have noted in appendices A–C.

Here, however, it is a question of the philosophy of the translators. In the case of the NIV, this philosophy has led to their having completely removed "hell" from the Old Testament!

King James Bible

DEU 32:22 For a fire is kindled in mine anger, and shall burn unto the **lowest hell**, and shall consume the earth with her increase, and set on fire the foundations of the mountains.

2SA 22:6 The **sorrows of hell** compassed me about; the snares of death prevented me;

JOB 11:8 It is as high as heaven; what canst thou do? **deeper than hell**; what canst thou know?

JOB 26:6 **Hell is naked** before him, and destruction hath no covering.

PSA 9:17 The wicked shall be **turned** into **hell**, and all the nations that forget God.

PSA 16:10 For thou wilt not leave my soul in **hell**; neither wilt thou suffer thine Holy One to see corruption.

PSA 18:5 The sorrows of **hell** compassed me about: the snares of death prevented me.

PSA 55:15 Let death seize upon them, and let them go down quick into **hell**: for wickedness is in their dwellings, and among them.

PSA 86:13 For great is thy mercy toward me: and thou hast delivered my soul from the **lowest hell**.

PSA 116:3 The sorrows of death compassed me, and the **pains of hell** gat hold upon me: I found trouble and sorrow.

New International Version

For a fire has been kindled by my wrath, one that burns to the **realm of death below**. It will devour the earth and its harvests and set afire the foundations of the mountains.

The **cords of the grave** coiled around me; the snares of death confronted me.

They are higher than the heavens— what can you do? They <u>are **deeper than the depths of the grave**</u>—what can you know?

Death is naked before God; Destruction lies uncovered.

The wicked return to the **grave**, all the nations that forget God.

because you will not abandon me to the **grave**, nor will you let your Holy One see decay.

The cords of the **grave** coiled around me; the snares of death confronted me.

Let death take my enemies by surprise; let them go down alive to the **grave**, for evil finds lodging among them.

For great is your love toward me; you have delivered me from the **depths of the grave**.

The cords of death entangled me, **the anguish of the grave** came upon me; I was overcome by trouble and sorrow.

PSA 139:8   If I ascend up into heaven, thou art there: if I make my bed in **hell**, behold, thou art there.

If I go up to the heavens, you are there; if I make my bed in the **depths**, you are there.

PRO 5:5 Her feet go down to death; her steps take hold on **hell**.

Her feet go down to death; her steps lead straight to the **grave**.

PRO 7:27 Her house is the way to **hell**, going down to the chambers of death.

Her house is a highway to the **grave**, leading down to the chambers of death.

PRO 9:18 But he knoweth not that the dead are there; and that her guests are in the depths of **hell**.

But little do they know that the dead are there, that her guests are in the depths of the **grave**.

PRO 15:11 **Hell** and destruction are before the LORD: how much more then the hearts of the children of men?

Death and Destruction lie open before the LORD — how much more the hearts of men!

PRO 15:24 The way of life is above to the wise, that he may depart from **hell** beneath.

The path of life leads upward for the wise to keep him from going down to the **grave**.

PRO 23:14 Thou shalt beat him with the rod, and shalt deliver his soul from **hell**.

Punish him with the rod and save his soul from **death**.

PRO 27:20 **Hell** and destruction are never full; so the eyes of man are never satisfied.

Death and Destruction are never satisfied, and neither are the eyes of man.

ISA 5:14   Therefore **hell** hath enlarged herself, and opened her mouth without measure: and their glory, and their multitude, and their pomp, and he that rejoiceth, shall descend into it.

Therefore the **grave** enlarges its appetite and opens its mouth without limit; into it will descend their nobles and masses with all their brawlers and revelers.

ISA 14:9   **Hell from beneath is moved** for thee to meet thee at thy coming: it stirreth up the dead for thee, even all the chief ones of the earth; it hath raised up from their thrones all the kings of the nations.

The grave below is all astir to meet you at your coming; it rouses the spirits of the departed to greet you— all those who were leaders in the world;...

ISA 14:15 Yet thou shalt be brought down to **hell**, to the sides of the pit.

But you are brought down to the **grave**, to the depths of the pit.

ISA 28:15 Because ye have said, We have made a covenant with death, and with **hell** are we at agreement;...

You boast, "We have entered into a covenant with death, with the **grave** we have made an agreement.

ISA 28:18 And your covenant with death shall be disannulled, and your agreement with **hell** shall not stand;

Your covenant with death will be annulled; your agreement with the **grave** will not stand...

ISA 57:9 ...and didst debase thyself even unto **hell**.

...you descended to the **grave** itself!

EZE 31:16 I made the nations to shake at the sound of his fall, when I cast him down to **hell** with them that descend into the pit:...

I made the nations tremble at the sound of its fall when I brought it down to the **grave** with those who go down to the pit...

EZE 31:17 They also went down into **hell** with him unto them that be slain with the sword;...

Those who lived in its shade, its allies among the nations, had also gone down to the **grave** with it, joining those killed by the sword.

EZE 32:21 The strong among the mighty shall speak to him out of the midst of **hell** with them that help him: they are gone down, they lie uncircumcised, slain by the sword.

From within the **grave** the mighty leaders will say of Egypt and her allies, 'They have come down and they lie with the uncircumcised, with those killed by the sword.'

EZE 32:27 And they shall not lie with the mighty that are fallen of the uncircumcised, which are gone down to **hell**...

Do they not lie with the other uncircumcised warriors who have fallen, who went down to the **grave**...

AMO 9:2 Though they dig into **hell** thence shall mine hand take them; though they climb up to heaven, thence will I bring them down:

Though they dig down to the **depths of the grave**, from there my hand will take them. Though they climb up to the heavens, from there I will bring them down.

JON 2:2 And said, I cried by reason of mine affliction unto the LORD, and he heard me; out of the **belly of hell** cried I, and thou heardest my voice.

He said: "In my distress I called to the LORD, and he answered me. From the **depths of the grave** I called for help, and you listened to my cry.

HAB 2:5 ...who enlargeth his desire as **hell**, and is as death, and cannot be satisfied, but gathereth unto him all nations, and heapeth unto him all people:

...Because he is as greedy as the **grave** and like death is never satisfied, he gathers to himself all the nations and takes captive all the peoples.

The word "hell" is present 22 times within the New Testament of the Authorized Bible compared to only 13 occurrences in the text of the New International Version. The real shock, however, is to see that this new popular translation **completely removes** the word from the Old Testament. Thus, there is no foundation in the Old upon which to build the doctrine in the New Testament.

Yes beloved, the modern versions of have gotten rid of the "thees" and "thous" – and much, much more!

Heaven and earth shall pass away:

but my words shall not pass away.

Mark 13:31

Section E
How Many Missing Words?

The most striking detail about the modern versions is that their New Testaments are clearly shorter than the Authorized King James Bible. The following depicts just how much shorter they are.

As translation from one language to another tends to expand or contract the number of words, an accurate picture would not be gained by merely counting the English words in the KJB, NIV or NASV. It is necessary to go to the Greek texts underlying these versions to obtain such. Even this will not yield a completely accurate count since a version will usually not follow one of the standard Greek editions at every point. However, the matter may be simplified by the realization that there are really only two kinds of Greek New Testaments – the Received Text and the Modern Critical Text. The Authorized (King James) Bible and all other Reformation Bibles were based on the former and practically all modern Bibles on the latter. We will not here examine their relative merits but will rather show book by book and chapter by chapter that the Critical Text is shorter.

The two most popular editions of the Critical Text are: The Nestle-Aland 26th Edition, and The United Bible Society 3rd Edition. These have a different format, but their text is identical. The most widely used edition of the Received Text was that prepared by Robert Stephanus in 1550. The KJB does not follow Stephanus in every instance, nor is the NIV text identical with the Nestle-Aland, but they are extremely close. Thus these two Greek Testaments provide a basis for comparison.

The following gives a chapter by chapter (in parenthesis) comparison of the Stephanus 1550 (number of words given first) and the Nestle-Aland 26th (the second number). Keep in mind that word omissions are only part of the story, there are also many word alterations in the modern version text.

MATTHEW

(1)	445 - 438	(2)	458 - 457	(3)	334 - 335	(4)	432 - 427
(5)	841 - 822	(6)	683 - 653	(7)	514 - 517	(8)	599 - 585
(9)	657 - 646	(10)	721 - 724	(11)	498 - 493	(12)	920 - 905
(13)	1096 - 1076	(14)	565 - 561	(15)	625 - 610	(16)	533 - 525
(17)	517 - 496	(18)	695 - 668	(19)	549 - 533	(20)	572 - 542
(21)	869 - 865	(22)	668 - 661	(23)	688 - 656	(24)	835 - 825
(25)	773 - 763	(26)	1274 - 1239	(27)	1036 - 1008	(28)	341 - 329

Total: 18,738 – 18,359 = 379 fewer words in the modern version text

MARK*

(1)	721 - 708	(2)	558 - 541	(3)	541 – 547	(4)	698 - 682
(5)	710 - 697	(6)	1017 - 981	(7)	631 - 605	(8)	644 - 630
(9)	914 - 858	(10)	919 - 885	(11)	595 - 563	(12)	837 - 793
(13)	637 - 606	(14)	1234 - 1197	(15)	689 - 667	(16)	301 - 308

Total: 11,646 – 11,268 = 378 fewer words in the modern version text

LUKE

(1)	1204 - 1186	(2)	864 - 849	(3)	594 - 585	(4)	799 - 767
(5)	760 - 754	(6)	957 - 924	(7)	913 - 890	(8)	1117-1086
(9)	1199 - 1151	(10)	808 - 782	(11)	1028 - 978	(12)	1059-1036
(13)	672 - 663	(14)	612 - 607	(15)	564 - 561	(16)	605 - 595
(17)	583 - 570	(18)	688 - 683	(19)	767 - 762	(20)	719 - 702
(21)	593 - 586	(22)	1113 - 1086	(23)	878 - 852	(24)	843 - 818

Total: 19,939 – 19,473 = 466 fewer words in the modern version text

JOHN*

(1)	844 - 829	(2)	434 - 430	(3)	671 - 658	(4)	952 - 946
(5)	830 - 792	(6)	1283 - 1241	(7)	871 - 861	(8)	1115-1070
(9)	698 - 692	(10)	711 - 695	(11)	985 - 944	(12)	888 - 892
(13)	668 - 665	(14)	592 - 580	(15)	499 - 500	(16)	601 - 581
(17)	512 - 499	(18)	804 - 779	(19)	821 - 821	(20)	627 - 614
(21)	551 - 547						

Total: 15,957 – 15,636 = 321 fewer words in the modern version text

*The modern versions either omit, place in the footnotes, question their authenticity, or place in brackets, Mark 16:9 – 20 and John 7: 53 – 8:11.

ACTS

(1)	511 - 506	(2)	848 - 839	(3)	504 - 506	(4)	682 - 687
(5)	787 - 771	(6)	280 - 280	(7)	1136 - 1113	(8)	723 - 695
(9)	812 - 786	(10)	872 - 837	(11)	533 - 528	(12)	496 - 501
(13)	954 - 932	(14)	481 - 472	(15)	716 - 694	(16)	723 - 721
(17)	677 - 673	(18)	528 - 511	(19)	766 - 756	(20)	694 - 676
(21)	814 - 798	(22)	584 - 567	(23)	676 - 662	(24)	495 - 459
(25)	539 - 530	(26)	597 - 596	(27)	748 - 755	(28)	618 - 597

Total: 18,794 – 18,448 = 346 fewer words in the modern version text

ROMANS

(1)	547 - 543	(2)	452 - 448	(3)	432 - 429	(4)	408 - 402
(5)	431 - 432	(6)	372 - 367	(7)	467 - 469	(8)	662 - 652
(9)	531 - 524	(10)	345 - 340	(11)	595 - 581	(12)	307 - 305
(13)	275 - 270	(14)	393 - 379	(15)	550 - 543	(16)	437 - 424

Total: 7,204 – 7,108 = 96 fewer words in the modern version text

I CORINTHIANS

(1)	502 - 501	(2)	293 - 288	(3)	347 - 341	(4)	347 - 345
(5)	231 - 220	(6)	344 - 335	(7)	690 - 686	(8)	227 - 225
(9)	452 - 450	(10)	484 - 463	(11)	538 - 531	(12)	475 - 471
(13)	199 - 196	(14)	624 - 608	(15)	852 - 847	(16)	328 - 323

Total: 6,933 – 6,830 = 103 fewer words in the modern version text

II CORINTHIANS

(1)	488 - 488	(2)	286 - 285	(3)	299 - 296	(4)	323 - 322
(5)	343 - 338	(6)	266 - 266	(7)	331 - 329	(8)	413 - 409
(9)	287 - 284	(10)	314 - 311	(11)	502 - 500	(12)	415 - 412
(13)	242 - 236						

Total: 4,509 – 4,476 = 33 fewer words in the modern version text

GALATIANS

(1)	362 - 364	(2)	383 - 386	(3)	464 - 454	(4)	451 - 445
(5)	319 - 314	(6)	272 - 267				

Total: 2,251 – 2,230 = 21 fewer words in the modern version text

EPHESIANS

(1)	404 - 401	(2)	362 - 362	(3)	337 - 325	(4)	486 - 483
(5)	472 - 457	(6)	401 - 393				

Total: 2,462 – 2,421 = 41 fewer words in the modern version text

PHILIPPIANS
(1)   499 - 501   (2)   434 - 431   (3)   349 - 340   (4)   359 - 357

Total: 1,641 – 1,629 = 12 fewer words in the modern version text

COLOSSIANS
(1)   552 - 538   (2)   403 - 388   (3)   378 - 369   (4)   288 - 286

Total: 1,621 – 1,581 = 40 fewer words in the modern version text

I THESSALONIANS
(1)   219 - 214   (2)   393 - 390   (3)   253 - 248   (4)   308 - 310
(5)   322 - 319

Total: 1,495 – 1,481 = 14 fewer words in the modern version text

II THESSALONIANS
(1)   237 - 235   (2)   319 - 310   (3)   278 - 274

Total: 834 – 819 = 15 fewer words in the modern version text

I TIMOTHY
(1)   310 - 306   (2)   190 - 186   (3)   209 - 207   (4)   225 - 221
(5)   336 - 328   (6)   354 - 343

Total: 1,624 – 1,591 = 33 fewer words in the modern version text

II TIMOTHY
(1)   318 - 317   (2)   361 - 358   (3)   238 - 236   (4)   337 - 327

Total: 1,254 – 1,238 = 16 fewer words in the modern version text

TITUS
(1)   253 - 251   (2)   190 - 189   (3)   223 - 219

Total: 666 – 659 = 7 fewer words in the modern version text

PHILEMON

Total: 339 – 334 = 5 fewer words in the modern version text

HEBREWS
(1)   255 - 256   (2)   321 - 313   (3)   281 - 283   (4)   292 - 291
(5)   234 - 232   (6)   303 - 301   (7)   459 - 456   (8)   283 - 274
(9)   509 - 512   (10)   559 - 550   (11)   639 - 633   (12) 479 - 474
(13) 376 - 378

Total: 4,990 – 4,953 = 37 fewer words in the modern version text

JAMES
(1)   411 - 406   (2)   428 - 416   (3)   300 - 295   (4)   278 - 277
(5)   346 - 348

Total: 1,763 – 1,742 = 21 fewer words in the modern version text

I PETER
(1)   415 - 409   (2)   395 - 393   (3)   378 - 370   (4)   322 - 305
(5)   214 - 207

Total: 1,724 – 1,684 = 40 fewer words in the modern version text

II PETER
(1)   385 - 384   (2)   376 - 374   (3)   343 - 341

Total: 1,104 – 1,099 = 5 fewer words in the modern version text

I JOHN
(1)   207 - 207   (2)   579 - 587   (3)   471 - 469   (4)   453 - 449
(5)   465 - 429

Total: 2,175 – 2,141 = 34 fewer words in the modern version text

II JOHN

Total: 249 – 245 = 4 fewer words in the modern version text

III JOHN

Total: 218 – 219 = 1 more word in the modern version text

JUDE

Total: 452 – 461 = 9 more words in the modern version

REVELATION
(1)   500 - 469   (2)   636 - 622   (3)   526 - 525   (4)   293 - 293
(5)   351 - 338   (6)   422 - 417   (7)   406 - 398   (8)   307 - 319
(9)   495 - 497   (10)   292 - 292   (11)   494 - 496   (12) 436 - 438
(13) 444 - 447   (14)   545 - 549   (15)   222 - 217   (16) 484 - 470
(17) 444 - 442   (18)   622 - 626   (19)   535 - 526   (20) 411 - 407
(21) 621 - 611   (22)   455 - 452

Total: 9,941 – 9,851 = 90 fewer words in the modern version text

SUB TOTAL: 140,523 – 137,976 = **2,547** *fewer words* in the modern version text.

However, after taking the two well-known passages of Mark 16:9–20 and John 7:53 – 8:11 into account, we obtain:

FINAL TOTAL: 140,523 – 137,601 = **2,922** *fewer words* in modern version text.

Thus, the modern version text is shorter in the New Testament than that of the King James Bible by about the total number of words contained in I and II Peter combined! Further, our first four sections have already depicted that these missing God-breathed words are usually extremely significant.

* * * * * * * * * * * * *

In closing this section, we add that Dr. Jay P. Green, a well known Greek and Hebrew scholar who has produced several Bible translations and a complete interlinear Bible in four volumes, has done the Church a great service in exposing the unfaithfulness of the New International Version (NIV).[1] Not only has the NIV committee selected the corrupt critical Greek text as its New Testament base, Dr. Green reveals that the translators were not even faithful in their rendering of it as they have left around 5 percent of the Greek words altogether **un-translated!** "A slightly lesser percentage" of the original Hebrew O.T. has been left un-translated (p. 120). Thus tens of thousands of God breathed words are not in the NIV.[2]

Moreover, they have added over 100,000 words without so signifying to the reader by placing such words in italics as did the Authorized King James translators. All 100,000[+] lack any Hebrew or Greek support whatever (pp. 120, 222–223).

---

[1] Jay P. Green, Sr. (ed.), *Unholy Hands on the Bible*, Vol. II, (Lafayette, IN: Sovereign Grace Trust Fund Pub., 1992), pp. 119–318.

[2] Thus clearly demonstrating that these translators did not consider the text to be God breathed.

Both Green and Dr. D.A. Waite[1] expose the NIV as being replete with free wheeling paraphrases rather than accurately rendering a translation. We trust the present author/editor's[2] work before the reader has likewise demonstrated beyond reasonable doubt the general untrustworthiness of the New International Version as well as all other versions that rely on the critical text as their foundation from which to translate.

---

[1] D.A. Waite *Defending the King James Bible*, (Collingswood, NJ: The Bible For Today Press, 1992). Dr. Waite "cut his teeth" on the Westcott-Hort Greek text at Dallas Theological Seminary (earning high A's) before the Nestle-Aland or United Bible Society Greek saw the light of day in its classrooms. He also sat at the feet of Bible Greek scholars while majoring in classical Greek and Latin at the University of Michigan. Twenty-one years later, he became persuaded through his own private study that the *Textus Receptus* was the true N.T. text.

Dr. Waite has acquired 66 semester hours in combined Classical and *Koine* Greek from the University of Michigan & Dallas Theological Seminary as well as 25 semester hours in Hebrew (he garnered all A's in both languages while at Dallas). This does not include his 8 semester hours of Latin, 8 semester hours of French, or 11 semester hours of Spanish. Thus, Dr. Waite has amassed a total of 118 semester hours (1,888 regular class hours) in foreign languages! Whatever differences the modern critics of the King James Bible and its underlying Hebrew and Greek texts may have with Dr. Waite, they cannot justifiably criticize his preparation and training in these essential disciplines.

Nor are Dr. Waite and Dr. Green alone in exposing this unfit translation; see for example: *The NIV Reconsidered* by Radmacher & Hodges; (Dallas, TX: Redencion Viva Pub., 1990) and Norman Ward, *Perfected or Perverted*, (Grand Rapids, MI: Which Bible Society).

[2] Over a 14-year professional career during which he held varying positions of responsibility as Paleontologist, Geophysicist, District Geophysicist, Geophysical Manager, and Regional Geophysicist with Texaco and Tenneco respectively, the author was selected to attend Division Manager School shortly before resigning from his scientific career in 1974 to pursue Biblical studies.

A magna cum laude graduate, Dr. Floyd Nolen Jones was awarded a teaching assistantship in geology by the University of Missouri. He later became the recipient of three National Science Foundation scholarships (Auburn Uni. & Uni. of Texas). Attaining the Ph.D. as well as a Th.D., Dr. Jones has garnered majors in the disciplines of Geology, Chemistry, Mathematics, Theology, and Education from six institutions of higher learning. An ex-evolutionist, he also possesses a minor in Physics and is an ordained Minister (SBC).

In addition to several published books in defense of the traditional biblical text, he has authored a published definitive work on bible chronology and an extensive analytical red-letter harmony of the Gospels. Having twice served as adjunct Professor at Continental Bible College in Brussels, Belgium, Dr. Jones is currently engaged in ongoing Biblical research, the public teaching of God's infallible Word as well as serving as Professor and Chairman of Biblical Chronology at Pacific International University. He and his wife, as well as his children and grandchildren, reside in Texas.

Whosoever therefore shall be ashamed of me
and of my words
in this adulterous and sinful generation;
of him also shall the Son of man be ashamed,
when he cometh in the glory of his Father
with the holy angels.

Mark 8:38

Section F
EPILOGUE

HOW DID SUCH RADICAL CHANGES COME ABOUT?

By now the perplexed inquirer must be wondering just how such radical changes have come about in the text of the Holy Scriptures.[1] Most have assumed that the majority of the differences have merely been the result of personal choices in the selection of differing synonyms and writing style. Such is not at all at the heart of the matter. We remind him of the many times he surely has heard or read from various sources words to the effect that "the oldest", "the best" or "the most reliable" manuscripts read so and so – or "omit" or "add" to the verses he has read. On and on the footnotes go in the various "Bibles" on the market today, crushing the faith of layman and pastor alike.

But how can they read so dramatically different in the relatively few yet numerically significant places that they diverge? After all, when the translators translate, it is understandable how one group may select different adjectives, conjunctions, synonyms etc., but our reader wonders – how can an entire word, indeed – a phrase, clause, sentence, verse and even a prolonged series of verses, be missing from one version to another? This is especially true when the King James (and all the many English versions prior to the KJB) is compared to all the newer versions. What is the basis for the many words which are present in the 1611 Authorized Version that are not to be found in these modern versions? Surely the 1611 translators did not just make them up out of thin air.

---

[1] Floyd Nolen Jones, *Which Version is The Bible,* 17th ed. revised & enlarged, (Houston, TX: KingsWord Press, 1999). All of this Epilogue has been gleaned from throughout this cited reference. *Which Version* is a detailed exposé and explanation relating to the problem under discussion. My friend and colleague Dr. Wilbur N. Pickering was the original source for much of the data on pages 56–60 [*What Difference Does It Make?*, (Dallas, TX: 1990)].

The ordinary reader naturally assumes that the changes have resulted from supposed advances made in the ongoing study of Greek which have sharpened the reviser's skill in translating. However, the shocking answer to these questions lies in the fact that there are two distinctly radically different Greek texts upon which the New Testament in English (or any other language) is based. Moreover, the Church for centuries has honored only one of these as the Holy Word of God. The other was rejected by the early Church during the 3rd to 5th centuries as a depraved Gnostic alteration of the true text. The early Church's rejection of this second text relegated it to an early grave. However, with the advent of modern archaeology and the so-called "sciences" of higher and lower text criticism, it has arisen inexplicably from its sandy Egyptian grave. Thus that which was rejected as a spurious, heretical text by the early Church and its successors down through the centuries is today being accepted as genuine. Strangely, in the past one hundred years, this "mummy" has been resurrected and once again has been offered to the Church as authentic – only this time the sleeping Church has not seen the danger. Yea, most are totally unaware that such an entity exists.

To better understand the problem surrounding the history of the New Testament Text, consider the circumstance whereby we wanted to make certain that a given copy of the American Constitution were perfectly accurate. We would simply compare it with the original hand-written document at the National Archives in Washington, D.C. However, such is not possible with the New Testament. All of its original manuscripts penned by Paul, Peter and other apostles in the first century A.D. have disappeared. Nearly all of the copies of these originals made during the early centuries thereafter were worn out, destroyed by the Roman Caesars, or remain undiscovered.

As a result of the discovery of a number of early manuscripts in the 19th century, questions arose concerning the original wording of the NT. Although these differed significantly in many places from the Traditional Greek text, many scholars concluded they were better copies of the originals because they were "older". This new approach led to Greek texts based largely upon a handful of early manuscripts.

The original manuscripts of the books of the New Testament were hand copied over and over again and copies were made from various generations of copies. As a result, numerous variant readings came to appear in New Testament manuscripts. Some of these were merely variations of spelling. Others were far more serious: (1) additions of words or phrases; (2) omissions of words, phrases, clauses, and whole sentences and paragraphs. These variant readings arose either from the inadvertent errors of copyists, or from the efforts of "scholars" (well-meaning or otherwise) to correct or even to improve the text.

It is the task of textual critics to ascertain just what the original reading was at every point in the New Testament text where a variant reading exists. This they do by sifting through a massive quantity of manuscript evidence, supposedly with great care. However, there are different schools of thought among textual critics, each with its own set of presuppositions and criteria for evaluating the authenticity of a reading and the relative importance of a given manuscript. Before accepting the conclusions of a particular textual critic, one should evaluate both his theological presuppositions and criteria.

The New Testaments of the King James Bible, William Tyndale's Bible, Luther's German Bible, Olivetan's French Bible, the Geneva Bible (English), as well as many other vernacular versions of the Protestant Reformation were translated from the Greek Text of Stephens, 1550, which (with the Elzevir Text of 1624) is commonly called the Textus Receptus, or the Received Text (TR). It is the "Traditional Text"[1] (T.T.) that has been read and preserved by the Greek Orthodox Church throughout the centuries. From it came the Peshitta, the Italic, Celtic, Gallic, and Gothic Bibles, the medieval versions of the evangelical Waldenses and Albigenses, and other versions suppressed by Rome during the Middle Ages. Though many copies were ruthlessly hunted down and destroyed, the Received Text has been preserved by an Almighty Providence.

This "Traditional Text" is also referred to as the "majority text",[2] since it is represented by about 95 percent of the manuscript evidence. This

---

[1] The Traditional Text (also referred to in the literature as "Syrian", "Byzantine" or the "majority" text) is an "identical twin brother" of the *Textus Receptus*. They are virtually identical in text and except for the infrequent instances where the T.T has missing text (i.e., I Joh.5:7–8; Acts 7:37, 8:37, 9:5–6; Luk.17:36; Mat.5:27, 27:35; Heb.2:7, 11:13 etc.), they exhibit only minor insignificant differences.

[2] Recently, several Greek NT's have been published under the designation "Majority Text". Therefore, in this epilogue the term "majority" is capitalized when referring to a single entity but is left in small letters when the word "majority" is intended with regard to the whole body of extant Greek manuscripts (i.e., as opposed to the "minority" of the mss).

is in sharp contrast to the Westcott-Hort tradition (which leans heavily on two manuscripts of the unreliable Alexandrian Text type), the shaky foundation of nearly all of today's versions. In the 16th century, Erasmus and the Reformers knowingly rejected the Gnostic readings of the Alexandrian Codex *Vaticanus* B and other old uncial (i.e., all capital letters with no spaces between words = MSS) manuscripts, whose variant readings they judged to be corrupt. They regarded such dubious "treasures" as the products of scribes who had altered the text to suit their own private interpretations. They also rejected Jerome's Latin Vulgate as a corrupt version and as an improper basis for vernacular translations.

The earliest known portion of the NT is Papyrus P-52 (until 1995 when the Magdalen Papyrus was dated as A.D. 66 & found to contain TR/KJB readings! See page 80). Also known as "John Rylands Greek 457", this 2.5 by 3.5 inch fragment is usually dated about A.D. 125 and contains John 18:31–33, 37–38. The earliest extant copy containing a complete book is Papyrus 72. Dated around 300, it contains all of I and II Peter and Jude. About 70 Greek MSS have been assigned a date earlier than 400 A.D., but almost all of them are very fragmentary. Where these do overlap, significant disagreement is usually found among them as to the correct wording. Around 190 Greek copies have been dated between A.D. 400–800. Most of these are also fragmentary, and they differ considerably where they overlap. As of 800 A.D., only eight extant Greek MSS contain all four gospels in essentially their entirety. Of these, only five contain all of Acts, five all of Romans and two all of Revelation.

Of the 3,000 plus Greek manuscripts of the NT, about 1700 are from the 12th – 14th centuries. They, along with 640 copies from the 9th to the 11th century, are in basic agreement on approximately 99% of the words of the NT. As a group, however, this majority disagree considerably with most of the copies from the early centuries – which also differ considerably among themselves.

This, then, is the situation that has given rise to the debate over the original wording of the New Testament. Nevertheless, despite all the variations, nearly all of the words of the NT enjoy over 99% attestation from the extant Greek MSS/mss. Only about 2% have less than 95% support and fewer than 1% of the words have less than 80% (and most of these differ only slightly).

Yet for the past 100 years, the world of scholarship has been dominated by the view that this majority text is a secondary and inferior text. Scholars have rejected that we have had the true text of the originals all along and have thus attempted to reconstruct the original text of the NT on the basis of the few early manuscripts. But as these copies differ considerably among themselves, the result has been an eclectic "patchwork quilt". The editors of the dominant eclectic Greek text of today have usually followed a single Greek MSS and in dozens of places they have printed a text not found in any known Greek copy! The discrepancy between this eclectic text and the majority reading is about 8%. That would amount to 48 full pages of discrepancies in a 600 page text. Around 1/5 of that represents omissions in the "minority text" such that it is about 10 pages shorter than the majority text. Nearly all modern versions of the Bible are based on this "minority text" whereas the King James is based on an identical twin brother of the "majority text". This is why so many verses, phrases, etc. familiar to users of the KJB are missing in the modern versions.

The question is which of these two Greek texts is the Word of God? There are a number of reasons for rejecting these early MSS as spurious. An inquiry reveals that the "majority text" has dominated the stream of transmission down through the centuries because the Church considered it to be the God given text. It has the greatest geographic distribution as well as the longest continuity throughout time. The "minority text" never circulated widely within the Church, and it virtually disappeared after the 4th century. Further, they have few direct descendants, demonstrating that they were rejected in their day – not deemed worthy of copying. The undisputed fact that the early minority copies not only differ from the majority but also differ significantly among themselves undermines their credibility as valid witnesses to the true text.

It is often stated that no matter what Greek text one may use no Christian doctrine is actually affected, hence, the whole controversy is but a "tempest in a teapot". Not so, for although as many as half of the differences between the "majority" and "minority" texts be termed "inconsequential", about 25 pages of significant discrepancies remain – and the "minority" omits words from the text that total 10 pages.

Moreover, the "minority text" has introduced some unequivocal errors which make the doctrine of inerrancy indefensible. For example, Matthew 1:7 and 1:10 list Asaph and Amos, two non-existent kings, in

Christ's genealogy whereas the Traditional Text correctly reads "Asa" and "Amon". Luke 23:45 has a scientific error in the Minority reading. Here it is stated that the sun was eclipsed (Gr. eklipontos) at Christ's death, but this is impossible as the Passover always occurs during the time of the full moon. An eclipse of the sun can occur only during the new moon phase. The T.T. reads "the sun was darkened" (eskotisthe). The Minority Text of John 7:8 relates Jesus' telling his brothers that He is not going to the feast; then two verses later, He goes. No contradiction exists in the T.T. which records Jesus as saying "I am not yet going".

The result of this is that although most major Christian doctrine is not at risk (though several such as eternal judgment, the ascension and the deity of Jesus are significantly weakened), two are. Total havoc is played upon the doctrine of Divine Inspiration due to the plain errors of fact and contradictions incorporated in the eclectic text of the NT. Divine inspiration becomes relative, and the doctrine of the Scriptures being the infallible deposit of God's Word to man becomes untenable.

Thus, modern scholarship has perniciously undermined the credibility of the New Testament text. This credibility crisis has been forced upon the attention of the laity by the modern versions that enclose parts of the text in brackets and add numerous footnotes that are often inaccurate and slanted which raise doubt as to the integrity of the text. Moreover, this credibility crises is being exported around the world through the translations and revisions of the NT that are based on the eclectic text.

Today, the Christian is being seduced and asked to believe in the "INSPIRATION" without believing in the "PRESERVATION" of the Scriptures. We are being asked to believe in the inspiration of the "originals" without believing in the preservation of the text of the Scriptures. It is a statement of unbelief when we say that we only believe that the original autographs were inspired. What we really are saying is that we do not believe that we have the infallible Word of God on this planet, or at least in our hands, at this moment.

THE 1881 REVISION COMMITTEE

But how did the problem of the two radically different Greek NT texts come to overwhelm the unsuspecting Christian Church? In 1881 A.D., part of the Church of England (Anglican) decided to revise the King

James Bible (the Authorized Version).[1] The Greek New Testament upon which this translation had been based was the result of years of study and work by the brilliant scholar, Desiderius Erasmus (1466– 1536 A.D.). Being satisfied with the King James Bible, the northern convocation of the Church of England did not want a revision. However, the southern convocation favored a change and proceeded alone.

A committee of Hebrew and Greek scholars was selected and was charged to change the obsolete spelling, update punctuations, change archaic words like "concupiscence" to "unholy desires", etc. and thus update the language. As the Southern convocation was content with the text itself, no real overhaul of the version was intended. All changes were to be of minor significance.

That is not what the committee did. The men composing the revision committee went against the directive which the Anglican Church had given them. Without authorization and in totally direct insubordination, rather than merely improve the *English* they produced *a radically different Greek text* – a very different New Testament! They did not use the Greek text upon which the King James was based. Cast aside as worthless were the Greek manuscripts upon which not only the King James but the many other English bibles which had preceded the King James had been based (i.e., the Great Bible, the Bishops' Bible, Matthew's, Geneva etc.). They thus produced an entirely different "Bible". This is one of the least known facts and greatest guarded secrets within the confines of Christendom. Few people, laymen or pastors, are aware of these happenings.

We must understand that if we have a version other than the King James, it has been based upon a Greek text different from the one used to produce the King James Bible. Thus, that which was named the "Revised" Version was not a revision! Instead, the committee altered the *original* Greek and *substituted a radically different Greek text* – introducing c.5,337 alterations – yet almost no one is cognizant of this!

From whence came this new Greek text? To answer and unravel this calls for a look into the past. Strengthen yourself gentle reader, that which follows is a dreadful account of compromise, deception, and betrayal – all directed against the Living God, His Word, and His people.

---

[1] Jasper J. Ray, *God Wrote Only One Bible,* (Junction City, OR: Eye Opener Pub., 1980), pp. 23–24.

ORIGEN ADAMANTIUS – THE FOUNTAINHEAD
OF THE PROBLEM

Origen compiled an Old Testament called the Hexapla (c.245 A.D.). It was, in effect, a parallel Bible which had six columns. The first column was the Hebrew Old Testament. Three other columns portrayed Greek translations by men who were Ebionites. They believed in the ethical teachings of Jesus but did not believe in Paul's doctrines of grace. Indeed, they called Paul an apostate and wholly rejected all his epistles.[1] They did not believe Jesus was Deity – that He was God with a capital "G", and taught that Joseph was the father of Jesus. Several of the Ebionites whose translations were included in these columns later apostatized, returning to Judaism.

One of them (Aquila of Sinope, 80–135 A.D.) was excommunicated from the Christian community for steadfastly refusing to give up astrology and for practicing necromancy.[2] He conjectured that the Greek word "*parthenos*" of Matthew 1:23 was not the Virgin Mary but represented a corruption in the original text. According to Aquila, the correct understanding was that Jesus was the bastard son of Mary and a blond Roman soldier of German extraction named "Pantheras" (Eng. = panther).[3] Origen considered these Ebionites works to be "inspired" and thus included them in his "Bible".

The fifth column (written in classical Greek) supposedly is Origen's revision of an older pre A.D. Greek Old Testament translation. Today, this 5th column is referred to by text critics (though they are loathe to admit this) as the "LXX" or the "Septuagint".[4]

Origen also worked with the New Testament. Whereas he mainly translated the Old, he *edited* the New. Origen traveled extensively and everywhere he found a Greek New Testament, it was altered to fit his

---

[1] Eusebius, *Ecclesiastical History*, 2 Vols., Loeb Classical Library, (Cambridge, MA: Harvard UP, 1980), Vol. 1, Bk III, ch. 27.

[2] Foy E. Wallace, *A Review of the New Versions,* (Ft. Worth, TX: Noble Patterson Pub., 1973), Addenda, section 3, p. 21. Wallace reprints Professor R.C. Foster's "The Battle of the Versions" in his Addenda, 3rd & 4th sections, pp. 13–36.

[3] *Ibid.,* Addenda, section 3, p. 17.

[4] Floyd Nolen Jones, *The Septuagint: A Critical Analysis*, 6th ed., rev. & enl., (Houston, TX: KingsWord Press, 1998), p. 17.

doctrine.   He, of course, felt that he was merely "correcting" the manuscripts. However, men of God do not change original manuscript readings. If one does not agree with the text of a manuscript, the place for change is at translation; but to alter the original document – never! Origen had a wealthy patron who supplied seven stenographers and seven copyists to accompany and assist him as he systematically altered Scripture.[1]

Origen was the third head master of a school in Alexandria, Egypt, which had been founded in 180 A.D. by the Greek philosopher Pantaenus.   Pantaenus was succeeded in 202 A.D. by Clement of Alexandria (not to be confused with Clement of Rome) who taught that Plato's work was also inspired in the same sense as Scripture. Their writings indicate they were lost, albeit "religious", Greek philosophers. Neither professed a new birth apart from water baptism; indeed, it was on the basis of their having been so baptized that they declared themselves "Christian".

ORIGEN'S BELIEFS

The following is a composite gleaned from many sources[2] depicting the beliefs of Origen. Let us examine them to see if he was in fact a "great early Father of the Church" as we are often told.

This Greek philosopher had been taught by the founder of Neo-Platonism (Ammonius Saccas 170–243 A.D.).   Neo-Platonism is a strange combination of Aristotelian logic and Oriental cult teachings. It conceives the world as being an emanation from "the one" – the impersonal one (not the personal "Abba" [Father or Daddy] of the Bible) with whom the soul is capable of being reunited while in some sort of trance or ecstasy.

As a follower of that philosophy, Origen attempted to amalgamate its views to Christianity. The problem with Origen, as with many who

---

[1] Elgin S. Moyer, *Who Was Who in Church History*, (Chicago, IL: Moody Press, 1962), p. 315; also John H. P. Reumann, *The Romance of Bible Scripts and Scholars*, (Englewood Cliffs, NJ: Prentice Hall, 1965), pp. 98–103 for a more detailed account.

[2] Albert Henry Newman, *A Manual of Church History*, (Valley Forge, PA: Judson Press, 1902), Vol. I, pp. 284–287; Herbert Musurillo, *The Fathers of the Primitive Church* (New York: Mentor-Omega Pub., 1966), pp. 31, 38, 195, 198, 202–203; *Encyclopedia Britannica*, Vol. 16, (1936 – esp. point 4, later editions omit this fact), pp. 900–902, to name but a few.

profess Christianity today, was that he tried to take "the best" of the world system (that which he had learned in school – his old philosophic views etc.) and incorporate them into Christianity; but they do not mix.

It will be noted that many of Origen's beliefs coincide with Roman Catholic and Jehovah's Witness doctrine, both of which are "Christian" cults. Origen believed:

1. in soul sleep (that the soul "sleeps" in the grave until the resurrection). However, the Bible teaches that to be absent from the body is to be present with the Lord (II Cor.5:8);

2. in baptismal regeneration (belief that one is saved by water baptism). Although Satan was the originator, Origen is the first man we can find who was a strong proponent of this doctrine;

3. in universal salvation, i.e., the ultimate reconciliation of **all** things including Satan and the demons;

4. that the Father was God with a capital "G" and Jesus was God with a little "g" – that Jesus was only a created being. Thus, Origen was not Christian in the most basic of all doctrine, namely the person of the Lord Jesus the Christ;

5. to become sinless, one had to go to purgatory . This doctrine is nowhere to be found in Scripture;

6. in transubstantiation (at communion the bread and wine actually turn to the body and blood of Christ);

7. in transmigration and reincarnation[1] of the soul. (The resurrection of Jesus corrects that error as He came back to life as **the same Jesus**. Hebrews 9:27 says "And it is appointed unto men **once** to die, but after this the judgment". Thus, the Bible teaches there is no reincarnation.);

---

[1] Transmigration means that one comes back to life as *something* else, i.e., a frog, or some other animal or even a tree. Reincarnation means that you come back to life as *someone* else – another human. Someone may reply "Well, reincarnation should be the case so that we can have a second chance". Such is heresy. Never should God give a "second chance". How terrible and wicked it would be of God to give *only* two opportunities to be saved! God has given every man during his lifetime literally hundreds and thousands of opportune moments to have his soul saved from the terrible consequences of sin, by simply receiving Jesus as his substitute – as his Lord and Savior.

8. and would not concede that any intelligent person could believe the temptations of Jesus as recorded in the Scriptures actually happened;[1]

9. the Scriptures were not literal (Origen was the "father of allegories");

10. neither in an actual "Adam" nor the fall of man and that Genesis 1–3 was not literal or historical;

11. the correct interpretation of Matthew 19 was that a man of God should be castrated and thereby proceeded to emasculate himself;[2]

12. and taught eternal life was not a gift, rather that one must seize hold on and retain it (but Eph.2:8 says "By faith are ye saved through grace; and that not of yourselves: it is the gift of God".);

13. that "Christ enters no man until he grasps mentally the doctrine of the consummation of the ages" (that would eliminate about 99.9% at most typical Christian gatherings);

14. or intimated that non baptized infants were hell bound; and

15. the redeemed would not experience a *physical* resurrection (yet I Cor.15 teaches a physical resurrection, as do many other Scriptures). Moreover, around 200 A.D. Alexandrian "Christians" taught that Mary was the second person of the Trinity ("Quarterly Journal of Prophecy" [July, 1852], p. 329).

---

[1] Origen went on to even correct Jesus, for in Matthew 13:38 in the parable of the sower Jesus says that the field is the world (Mat.13:34). Origen said "the field was Jesus". Later, he changed his mind, deciding that the field was the Scriptures.

[2] In so doing, Origen mutilated that which supposedly was the temple of the Holy Spirit. Jesus was not so teaching. When Jesus gave an example about plucking out an eye or cutting off a hand rather than to enter hell – He was teaching how dreadful sin was, how terrible hell was and with how radically sin had to be dealt. Jesus knew that no man in his right mind would really pluck out his eye or cut off his hand. Jesus was speaking to that person who would rationalize and say "Oh, I didn't want to do it. I did not want to gaze at her with an adulterous eye but my eye just did so. I didn't want to seize the money but my hand simply took it. I am basically a fine person. The problem is that my hand (or eye, he, she or even the devil) made me do it. Anybody, everybody but it is not my fault!" Jesus was saying in effect – Oh, if that is the case, simply cut off your hand or pluck out your eye.

Jesus desired to jar mankind out of its complacent self-satisfied lifestyle into an honest appraisal of the situation to the intent that they might repent. Again, He knew that they would not really pluck out their eyes nor did He mean for them to do so. He was teaching the horror and reality of hell. In Matthew 12 and 15 and in Jeremiah 17:9, Jesus taught that sin was a matter of the heart. One can pluck out an eye or cut off a hand but still think about and long to sin (compare the Baalite priest's cutting their flesh so as to gain their god's attention in I Ki.18:28 – self-mutilation is purely pagan).

Origen is often depicted as a "man of God", especially because he "*died for his beliefs*". That is certainly a commendable character trait, but Mussolini, Karl Marx and Hitler also died for their beliefs. That does not mean they were Christians. Many people have believed in a cause enough to give their lives for it, but it does not follow that they were Christian. Origen's beliefs clearly show that he was a religious Gnostic Greek philosopher and not truly a born again son of God.

The question that must be faced is – would a man who fits the spiritual description of Origen as outlined on the two previous pages (whose work Westcott & Hort used) ever produce a faithful text?

WHAT ARE THE MATERIALS AVAILABLE TODAY?[1]

It might be well to begin by considering what manuscript evidence is available today as to the true text of the New Testament. We have *no* New Testament manuscripts which are complete. We only have pieces, fragments, chapters, books etc. Until 1995, no first century manuscripts of the New Testament had been discovered (see page 80). We have 88 Greek papyri manuscripts. The papyri are of newspaper type quality, usually rolled but sometimes in book form. Most papyri consist of small fragments and thus do not exhibit much text. Of the 88, only an estimated thirteen (15%) support *Vaticanus* B and *Sinaiticus Aleph* which are the two foremost manuscripts supporting the above mentioned radical new Greek text; about seventy-five (c.85%) support the Greek Received Text upon which the King James was founded (hereafter designated "TR").[2]

We have 267 Greek Uncials (text written in capital letters, also called "majuscules", designated by "MSS"), none of which is complete. Pages, chapters, and even books are missing. Of course some are in much better condition than others. Only nine of these support the Westcott-

---

[1] Kurt Aland, "The Greek New Testament: Its Present and Future Editions", *Journal of Biblical Literature*, LXXXVII (June, 1968), p. 184. Aland is Europe's leading textual critic and director of the center at Munster, West Germany where c.80% of the extant Greek MSS, mss and papyri are stored on microfilm. At the writing of his book, Aland listed 81 papyri; however, a few more have been located since the 1968 publication cited here, bringing the total to 88.

[2] D.A. Waite, *Defending the King James Bible*, (Collingswood, NJ: The Bible For Today Press, 1992), p. 54.

Hort critical text upon which the new radical Greek text[1] was based (merely 3%) whereas 258 (97%) support the Greek Received Text.[2]

There are 2,764 Greek cursive manuscripts (written in small letters, designated by "mss"), often called "minuscules". Thus most of the Greek witnesses to the true text of the New Testament are the Greek cursives. Merely twenty-three (1%) sustain the W-H readings which are the Greek foundation of nearly all the modern translations while 2,741 (99%) uphold the Received Text.[3]

We also have 2,143 Greek lectionaries (from a Latin root meaning "to read", manuscripts containing Scripture lessons which were read publicly in the churches from at least A.D. 400 until the time of the invention of printing).[4] All (100%) of them support the Received Text which underlies the King James Bible.[5] This gives us a total of 5,262 Greek witnesses to the true text of the New Testament of which 5,217 or ninety-nine percent are in agreement. This group dates from the fifth century on. The remainder not only disagree with the 99% majority – but disagree among themselves. Nevertheless, these few have controlled the camp of academia for the past one hundred years. The question, of course, is how can this be – how did such come to happen?[6]

It is true that several thousand mss have been discovered since 1611. This is the major factor that has been used to justify to the church at large the need for a major revision of the King James. It seems logical that if a vast amount of data not available to the King James translators has been brought to life – these new materials must be considered. This especially seems reasonable as some of these mss were dated between 350–380 A.D. whereas Erasmus' five mss were from the 10th to 15th centuries. Admittedly this rhetoric seems very

---

[1] The modern expression of this radical text is found in the highly lauded UBS[3] and Nestle[26] editions.

[2] Waite, *Defending the King James Bible, op. cit.*, p. 55.

[3] *Ibid.*, p. 55

[4] John W. Burgon, *The London Quarterly Review*, (October): 1881.

[5] Waite, *Defending the King James Bible, op. cit.*, p. 55.

[6] Again, for a more detailed and fully documented answer, the reader is encouraged to see: Jones, *Which Version is The Bible, op. cit.*

compelling. However, of the several thousand manuscripts discovered since 1611, the great majority (90–95%) **agree** with the Greek text of those five mss which Erasmus used. Nevertheless, the new translations are rife with footnotes informing the reader that "the oldest, the best manuscripts read such and such" as opposed to the King James. But is it not devastating to realize that what has been kept from the church at large is the fact that the vast majority (c.90–95%) of these more recent finds read the same as the Traditional Text which underlies the Reformers Bibles and the King James translation?

Only less than 3% of the text does not agree with 90% of the MSS.[1] Furthermore, we are not judging between two text forms of, say 90% versus 10%. **As the minority disagree among themselves** (Only B and P-75 agree closely[2]), *the percentage is more like 90% versus 1%.* For example, in I Tim. 3:16 which the King James renders as:

> And without controversy great is the mystery of godliness: ***God was manifest*** in the flesh, ...

Over 300 mss read "God was manifest", only 8 mss say something else; of those 8, five say "who" instead of "God" and three have private interpretations – which is 97% versus 2%. Yet, since Westcott and Hort, critics have adopted the Alexandrian reading "who was manifest in the flesh" as preserved in *Aleph* (ℵ) and have translated the word "who" as "He who", all the while insisting that Paul is quoting here from a fragment of an early Christian Hymn.[3] Thus, according to the critics, Paul quoted an incomplete sentence, one having a subject without a predicate and even that has been left dangling.[4] I think not!

Let us now consider the current status of the Mark 16:9–20 passage. Most modern versions have a footnote to the effect that "these verses

---

[1] Wilbur N. Pickering, *The Identity of the New Testament Text,* (Nashville, TN: Thomas Nelson, 1977), p. 112.

[2] But P-75 cannot be regarded as a guarantee that B's text is of the 2nd century. It is unjustified to conclude from the agreements between P-75 and B in portions of Luke and John that the whole NT text of B is reliable. There also exists a sufficiently large number of disagreements between the two which must be deemed as important as the agreements.

[3] Edward F. Hills, *The King James Version Defended,* 4th ed., (Des Moines, IA: Christian Research Press, 1984), p. 138.

[4] *Ibid.*

are not in the oldest, best, most reliable Greek manuscripts". In laymen's terms this means that Mark 16:9–20 are not in the two 4th century Greek manuscripts, *Vaticanus* B and *Sinaiticus Aleph* which were derived from Origen's (185–254) edited New Testament (a 12th century minuscule also omits the verses). Satan has always wanted to strip the church of its power, authority, and commission. These verses are the Great Commission spoken by Jesus as recorded by Mark. It is an apostolic commission delegating great power to the body of Christ that it may continue the ministry of the Lord Jesus.

Of the approximately 3,119 Greek manuscripts of the NT extant today, none is complete. The segment of text bearing Mark 16 has been lost from many, but over 1,800 contain the section and verses 9–20 are present in all but the 3 cited above.[1] The footnote is thus unveiled and laid bare as dishonest and deliberately misleading in intimating that these verses are not the Word of God.

The external evidence is massive. Not only is the Greek manuscript attestation ratio over 600 to 1 in support of the verses (99.99%), around 8,000 Latin mss, about 1,000 Syriac versions as well as all of the over 2,000 known Greek Lectionaries contain the verses.[2] They were cited by Church "Fathers" who lived 150 years or more *before* B or *Aleph* were written e.g.: Papias (c.100), Justin Martyr (c.150), Tatian (c.175), Irenaeus (c.180), and Hippolytus (c.200). Further, the Vatican MSS has a blank space exactly the size required to include the 12 verses at the end of the 16th chapter. The scribe who prepared B obviously knew of the existence of the verses and their precise content. Indeed, as Tischendorf observed, *Sinaiticus* exhibits a different handwriting and ink on this page, and there is a change in spacing and size of the individual letters in an attempt to fill up the void left by the removal of the verses. These circumstances testify that the sheet is a forgery.

Do we really believe that God would have the greatest story ever told end at verse 8: "And they went out quickly, and fled from the

---

[1] Even in 1871 A.D., 620 of the then extant mss were known to contain Mark 16; **only** *Vaticanus* B and *Sinaiticus Aleph* did not have verses 9–20; John W. Burgon, *The Last Twelve Verses of the Gospel According to S. Mark*, (Oxford and London: James Parker & Co., 1871), p. 71. Since 1871, hundreds more of the 3,119 mss have been discovered.

[2] Only one Latin mss, one Syriac and one Coptic version omit Mark 9–20. Much of the material in this paragraph has been gleaned from Dr. Wilbur N. Pickering's taped interview before the Majority Text Society in Dallas, Texas (Summer of 1995).

sepulcher; for they trembled and were amazed: neither said they any thing to any man; for they were afraid". Would God allow the good news of the Gospel to end with his disciples cringing in fear? Would Mark conclude his Gospel without any reference to the appearance of the risen Christ to His disciples? Hardly! The reader should feel a deep sense of righteous anger upon learning of the unscrupulous manner in which these verses have been presented by various publishers.

The reader must come to realize that the new Bible translations appeal, not because they are faithful to the original text, but because they have placed the ability to *communicate* over and above fidelity to the actual Words of God. The obvious reason for this being foisted upon the public is – greed for money.

The majority of modern Bible publishers (not to be confused with Bible Societies) are neither religious organizations nor missionary societies deserving our unqualified trust.[1] Operating in the cold hard world of business, they care not whether their product is a faithful rendering of the true text. Their interest lies along the lines of profit. They are not after the souls of men unto salvation or edification; rather it is their purchasing power which attracts these companies. Tragically, the same is true concerning most owners of "Christian" book stores who sell not only any translation but paperbacks and commentaries espousing nearly every wind of doctrine. The reason this continues year after year at a more maddening pace is – itching ears for winds of doctrine (II Tim.4:3–4; Eph.4:14). The circle is ever widening and vicious.

Equally distressing is that the numerous modern translations are being sponsored and/or produced by publishing companies and by individuals who answer to no ecclesiastical arm of the Church. There is no one to whom they are accountable. Thus faithfulness to accurate translation is of little consequence to most of them. The criteria has become readability rather than correctness, and after a Madison Avenue sales promotion advertising the product as "easy to under-stand" or "reads just like today's newspaper", the final criteria and motive become that of profit.

---

[1] *Tindale's Triumph, John Rogers' Monument*, The New Testament of the Matthew's Bible 1537 A.D., John Wesley Sawyer, ed., (Milford, OH: John the Baptist Printing Ministry, 1989), p. iv; from the forward written by Dr. Theodore P. Letis.

BACK TO THE 1881 REVISION COMMITTEE

Let us now return back to the 1881 Revision Committee and examine the lives (and the text which they produced) of two of its leading members – Westcott and Hort. These two men had been working in secret prior to the revision for over twenty years putting together a theretofore unpublished Greek text of the New Testament which was based almost exclusively upon one manuscript, *Vaticanus* B. Their New Testament altered the 140,521 word text of the *Textus Receptus* at 5,604 places involving 9,970 Greek words.[1] Representing 7 percent of the total word count, these 9,970 included Greek words that were either added, subtracted, or changed.

The new translations profess to be **revisions** of the 1611 King James. They are <u>not</u> for *they are not even from the same Greek text.* A radically different Greek New Testament was produced and has been used as the foundation for the new translations. We have had a new "bible" foisted upon us which is not a Bible at all for God authored only **ONE** Bible.

The Westcott-Hort Greek text contains about 5,788 departures from the Greek text of the *Textus Receptus.*[2] There are about 40 major omissions. These omissions deal with the virgin birth, the bodily resurrection, the deity of Jesus, and Jesus' authority. The readings of the 1611 King James translation are supported by third and fourth century Western and Byzantine manuscripts which are of the **same age** as *Vaticanus* B and *Aleph.* The *Textus Receptus* exalts Jesus in about ten passages in which the others tend to disparage and detract from Him. Out of the nearly 8,000 verses in the New Testament, 152 contain doctrinal corruptions in the W-H text.

Is it not incredulous that we are expected to believe God would allow the true text to sink into oblivion for fifteen hundred years only to have it brought to light again by two Cambridge professors who did not believe it to be verbally inspired?[3] As we read over the work of

---

[1] Waite, *Defending the King James Bible, op. cit.*, pp. 41–42. Dr. Jack Moorman, former professor at a Bible College in S. Africa & now pastor in London, personally counted every word in the TR, and Dr. Waite numerated the 5,604 changes made in it by W-H.

[2] Sir Frederick Kenyon, *Our Bible and the Ancient Manuscripts*, 5th ed. (London: Eyre & Spottiswoode, 1958), pp. 312–313.

[3] D.O. Fuller (ed.), *Which Bible?*, 3rd ed., (Grand Rapids, MI: International Pub., 1972), p. 149.

Westcott and Hort, one thing noticeable is the entire lack of their consideration of a supernatural element with regard to the Scriptures.[1] Thus having actually disavowed the doctrine of verbal inspiration and the overshadowing hand of God on His Word, their writings contain no sense of the divine preservation of the text, a doctrine which should be present in Christian deliberations.

THE NESTLE GREEK TEXT

Based upon the Westcott and Hort NT, the text of Eberhard Nestle (or the Aland-Nestle[26] or the third edition of the United Bible Society [UBS[3]], both of which are founded on the Nestle text and are almost identical to it), is being used today as the Greek New Testament in most of the seminaries. It contains about four changes per verse when compared to the *Textus Receptus*. Incredibly, we are told this does not affect a single Christian doctrine. But it does – it creates doubt in the minds of even the most devout that they really have an infallible Bible in their hands. It devastates the Christian's faith that the Bible is really the Word of God.

Eberhard Nestle's Greek text has 36,191 changes in the New Testament from the *Textus Receptus*. The resulting text would hardly read as the same book! Yet, it has to do so up to a point. The new translations read differently in some places but not everywhere. What if someone found an ancient Greek text out in the woods or in a cave? Would it be accepted as a genuine New Testament manuscript? What would be the hallmark, the criterion, the standard against which it would be measured? Believe it or not, after all we have said concerning the textual critics' negative views of the TR – it is nevertheless the standard by which all other manuscripts are measured. The new-found ms would have to agree 90% with the *Textus Receptus* to be considered legitimate.

We are always seeing footnotes (such as the Great Commission as given in Mark 16 and many other passages) that inform us that "the oldest, best, most reliable, most trustworthy, manuscripts read differently". What this means in simple language is, according to the scholars, an "untrustworthy manuscript" is one written on poor quality paper in the handwriting of a non-professional scribe.

---

[1] Fuller, *Which Bible?, op. cit.*, p. 165.

A "trustworthy" manuscript is one written on high quality paper or vellum and obviously prepared by highly educated professional scribes or scholars in neat capital letters – despite the fact that there may be many misspellings and omissions. However, they are referring to less than ten manuscripts and almost always only two – *Vaticanus* B and *Sinaiticus Aleph* (א).

An example, as already noted, is Mark 16:9–20 where many Bibles contain a very dishonest footnote which states that the oldest and most reliable Greek MSS do not contain these verses. As noted on page 58, we have over 3,000 NT Greek manuscripts, none of which is complete – neither does any contain all four of the gospels in their entirety. Over 1,800 contain Mark 16:9–20 and *only three do not*.[1] So you see, the footnote is both very dishonest and misleading. As mentioned previously, *Vaticanus* even has a space left exactly the size of those verses. More than ninety-nine percent of the Greek manuscripts have those verses; they are THE WORD OF GOD.

Of course everyone would like to have the readings taken directly from the original manuscripts, but they are no longer in existence. So far, there have not been found any autographs of the New Testament surviving today. This we deem to be the wisdom of God for surely we would have made them idols as the children of Israel did with the serpent of brass which Moses had made nearly 800 years earlier (II Ki. 18:4). Hezekiah had to destroy the brazen serpent because the people began to worship it instead of the God who had delivered them from the plague. People would do the same today – worship the paper instead of the God about whom it was written. We do not worship the Bible. We worship and serve the living God of whom it speaks.

THE TRUTH CONCERNING THE PAPYRI

The papyri (around 200 A.D.), which dates 150 years before *Vaticanus* and *Sinaiticus*, support the *Textus Receptus* readings. This may come as somewhat of a shock to those familiar with the problem of textual criticism, as most have been informed that the early papyri are

---

[1] Again, this was gleaned from Dr. Wilbur N. Pickering's taped interview before the Majority Text Society in Dallas, Texas (Summer 1995). In Burgon's day (1871 A.D.), 620 of the then extant mss contained Mark 16; **only** *Vaticanus* B and *Sinaiticus Aleph* did not have verses 9–20, Burgon, *The Last Twelve Verses of the Gospel According to S. Mark, op. cit.*, p. 71.

classified as Alexandrian or Western text-types. True, nevertheless the Chester Beatty and Bodmer Papyri, even though placed in those families, have many renderings which are strictly Syrian – strictly *Textus Receptus.* After a thorough study of P[46], Gunther Zuntz concluded: "A number of Byzantine readings, most of them genuine, which previously were discarded as 'late', are anticipated by P[46]".[1] Having several years earlier already acknowledged that with regard to the Byzantine New Testament "Most of its readings existed in the second century",[2] Colwell noted Zuntz's remark and concurred.[3] Many of these readings had been considered to be "late readings", but the papyri testify that they date back at least to the second century!

In his recent book, the late (d.1989) Harry A. Sturz[4] surveyed "all the available papyri" to determine how many papyrus-supported "Byzantine" readings were extant. In deciding which readings were "distinctively Byzantine", Dr. Sturz states that he made a conscious effort to "err on the conservative side" and thus his list is shorter than it could have been. Sturz lists 150 Byzantine readings which, though not supported by the early Alexandrian and Western uncials, are present in the bulk of later manuscripts <u>and</u> by the early papyri. Sturz lists a further 170 additional Byzantine readings which also read differently from the ℵ-B text but are supported by Western manuscripts. These are also supported in the ancient papyri. This

---

[1] Gunther Zuntz, *The Text of the Epistles,* (London: Oxford University Press, 1953), page 55.

[2] E.C. Colwell, *What is the Best New Testament?* (Chicago: The University of Chicago Press, 1952), p. 70.

[3] E.C. Colwell, "The Origin of Texttypes of New Testament Manuscripts", *Early Christian Origins,* ed. Allen Wikgren, (Chicago, IL: Quadrangle Books, 1961), p. 132.

[4] Harry A. Sturz, *The Byzantine Text-Type And New Testament Textual Criticism* (Nashville, TN: Thomas Nelson, 1984) pp. 61–62, 145–159. For many years Chairman of the Greek Department (contra the dust cover of his book) at Biola University, Dr. Sturz studied New Testament textual criticism with E.C. Colwell. This work is a slightly revised version of his doctoral dissertation at Grace Theological Seminary. Dr. Sturz passed away 26 April, 1989. Dr. Theodore P. Letis, who was literally tutored privately at the feet of Dr. E.F. Hills, states in a 7-20-88 critique of Sturz's book that Hills was the first text critic to use the papyri to vindicate Burgon's argument that the Byzantine text reached back well before the 4th-century. Letis relates that while a doctoral student under E.C. Colwell at the University of Chicago in 1942, Hills proposed a dissertation topic which – had it been accepted – would have accomplished that which Sturz set out to do 25 years earlier. The proposal was refused, hence Hills wrote his dissertation on another topic.

support may seem minimal, but nothing can diminish the fact that the total number of papyri citations favor the so-called "late" Byzantine readings against their rivals in the two lists by ***two to one***.[1] Sturz demonstrates papyri support for a total of 839 readings which in varying degrees would be classified as Byzantine. This forever dismantles Hort's theory that the Byzantine text was created as an official compromise text during the 4th-century by combining readings from earlier text-types.[2]

Dr. E.F. Hills declared that the Chester Beatty readings vindicate "distinctive Syrian readings" twenty-six times in the Gospels, eight times in the Book of Acts, and thirty-one times in Paul's Epistles.[3]

---

[1] Jack A. Moorman, *When The KJV Departs From The "Majority" Text*, (Collingswood, NJ: Bible For Today Press, #1617, 1988), p. 2.

[2] Hort proposed that in the early church of the third and fourth century, the Alexandrian, Neutral, and Western translations were competing with each other for acceptance. Hort promulgated the theory that an *official* text had been created by the church with ecclesiastical backing for the purpose of resolving the conflict, it having been completed by the middle of the fourth century (c.350 A.D.): B.F. Westcott & F.J.A. Hort, *Introduction to the New Testament in the Original Greek*, (NY: Harper & Bros., 1882), p. 133.

Westcott and Hort postulated that this text was a deliberate creation by scholarly Christians for the purpose of producing a text in which the readings reflected a compromise to end the turmoil over which of the three competing texts should be accepted as authoritative. They proposed that the Traditional Text was the product of an "official revision" (or "recension") of the New Testament which supposedly took place at Antioch in two stages between 250 and 350 A.D. (*Introduction, op. cit.*, pp. 137–138.) Thus their theory was that the T.T. had ecclesiastical backing for the purpose of constructing a text on which all could agree, and that it was because of this official backing that it overcame all rival texts and ultimately became the standard New Testament of the Greek Church. Hort portrayed Lucian (Bishop of Antioch, died 311 A.D.) as its probable initiator and overseer.

Thus Westcott and Hort advanced that it was the early Christians themselves who deliberately altered the Biblical text for the purpose of making Jesus appear more God-like, more divine! This vacuous and specious proposal borders on the preposterous. Holding literally that there is a curse from God on anyone who dares to so do, a genuine Christian (believing as he would in the infallibility of God's Word and in God's promises to preserve that same Word) would fear altering the Holy Text (Deu.4:2, 12:32; Proverbs 30:5–6; Psalm 12:6–7 and Revelation 22:18–19.). Indeed, **Lucian was an *Arian*** – an outspoken one – and NEVER would have favored readings exalting and deifying Jesus (Pickering, *The Identity of the New Testament Text, op. cit.*, p. 90). The hard fact is there is not one mention of such an ecclesiastical revision in all history.

[3] John W. Burgon, *The Last Twelve Verses of the Gospel According to S. Mark*, (Ann Arbor, MI: The Sovereign Grace Book Club, 1959), p. 50. This is a reprint of Burgon's

Hills goes on to state that Papyrus Bodmer II (Papyri 66) confirms 13% of the so-called "late" Syrian readings (18 out of 138).[1] To properly appreciate this one must consider the fact that only about thirty percent of the New Testament has any papyri support, and much of that thirty percent has only one papyrus.[2]

Thus this is seen as a major confirmation to the antiquity of the text of the Traditional Text in direct contradiction to the theory previously outlined in which the Syrian readings were said by W-H to be 4th or 5th century. May we not reasonably project that subsequent discoveries of papyri will give similar support to readings now only extant in Byzantine text?

TEXTUAL CRITICISM IS NOT SCIENTIFIC

Furthermore, textual criticism is not "scientific" because over the years nearly all of its leading proponents have systematically ignored the massive contrary evidence, refusing to give serious consideration to the objections, questions, and deliberations of the men who present such hostile testimony against their liberal views. It is not scientific because it continues to scorn and disregard the vast majority of manuscript data even though the supposed justification for so doing, the late text hypothesis and that of the Antiochian recension,[3] has been completely exposed as untrue and baseless.

Indeed, the notable works of Burgon, Miller, Hoskier, Scrivener, Hills, Pickering, and others who have championed the antithetical position have yet to obtain the hearing they deserve; yet such should be found in a truly open "scientific" forum where the supposed objective is to examine *all* the data and arrive at the truth. Today, extremely few Greek New Testament students have ever heard of these men, other than perhaps a few aside derogatory remarks such as "Burgon was the champion of lost causes", much less seen a copy of their works or actually read them.

Yet Burgon, despite his witticisms and taunts, presented innumerable documented hard facts and in so doing followed along a true scientific

---

1871 work containing an Introduction by Dr. Edward F. Hills, pp. 17–72.

[1] Burgon, *The Last Twelve Verses of the Gospel According to S. Mark, op. cit.*, p. 54.

[2] Pickering, *The Identity of the New Testament Text, op. cit.*, p. 77.

[3] See footnote 2, page 75.

approach much more so than did Westcott and Hort who, lacking hard proof, often resorted to fanciful imagination. Nevertheless W&H have been allowed a full hearing and attracted a large following. And why is this so? Part of the answer may be seen in Hoskier's remark: "The reason is sadly obvious, the latter method is taken easy, and at first sight plausible to the beginner. The former is horribly laborious, although precious in results".[1]

Moreover, the undeniable truth, as Letis has been documenting for the past several years, is that textual criticism leads to higher criticism which inevitably leads to the rejection of the historical and miraculous in the Word of God. Further, the 18th-century myth that "text criticism does not affect doctrine or the fundamental truths of Christianity" seizes, mesmerizes, and seduces all who have been formally instructed at educational institutions of higher learning, especially those who have attained advanced theological training.[2] Indeed, it is precisely the denial of *these* points that has lead to the destruction of the faith of many of today's pastors and priest with regard to the written Word of the Living God and has, since about the turn of the century, allowed for the free promotion of the modern translations which are all founded on the critical (eclectic) text.

Kenyon's words: "It is true (and cannot be too emphatically stated) that none of the fundamental truths of Christianity rests on passages of which the genuineness is doubtful"[3] are simply naive in the extreme as well as untrue. Regardless of the eminence of whosoever utters Kenyon's sentiment – it is a deception devoid of truth. Again, the plain errors of fact and contradictions incorporated in the eclectic text of the New Testament invalidates the doctrine of Divine Inspiration as it thereby becomes relative as well as rendering untenable the doctrine of the Scriptures as being the infallible deposit of God's Word to man.

Finally, this author concludes with Hoskier that without a *demonstrable* history of the transmission of the text (sans flights of the imagination) as well as an understanding of the interaction of the

---

[1] Herman C. Hoskier, *Concerning the Text of the Apocalypse* (2 Vols., London: Bernard Quaritch, Ltd., 1929), Vol. I, p. xlvii.

[2] Letis, in 1-12-1992, 4-6-1992 and 3-17-1993 correspondence from Edinburgh, Scotland.

[3] Kenyon, *Our Bible And The Ancient Manuscripts, op. cit.,* pp. 3–4; also see p. 55 in the 1958 edition for a similar remark.

versions upon each other and upon the Greek texts, text criticism can never be said to rest on a "scientific" foundation.[1] Indeed, Hoskier stated that it was this lack of scientific basis in the field of textual criticism that most concerned Dean John W. Burgon.[2]

NO FURTHER EFFORTS ARE NECESSARY TO PRODUCE GOD'S WORD

Indeed, by faith we know that we do not have to wait for any meticulous, lengthy undertaking to be completed in order for us to finally possess the original text. By faith, the child of God knows that he *already* has the Word of God at his disposal. A study of the history of the transmission of the Scriptures from their having been deposited by the Lord into the hands of man will further serve to strengthen that faith; yet such a study will not completely prove beyond all doubt that this is so.

This cannot be over emphasized, for unless we come by faith to a commitment that God has kept His promises and providentially preserved His Word in the *Textus Receptus* itself and not merely in the Greek majority readings, the final form of the text will forever be unsettled in our hearts.[3] The natural, rational mind resents this method. However the pitfalls apart from such a theological approach are many and dangerous.

Indeed, if we *only* used the majority concept as our standard, we would remain in constant uncertainty – in a state of flux. Who knows but on the morrow the archaeologist's spade may uncover an ancient library containing hundreds or even several thousands of Greek manuscripts embodying the "Alexandrian" text? Thus, the true reading would always hang in doubt for still later another library may be discovered with "Western" readings or even "Syrian". But we need not be concerned, for God has not left us depending upon the spade of the archaeologist to determine the true text. Neither are we awaiting his discovering a new papyri hiding in a jar somewhere. If we did so, our

---

[1] Herman C. Hoskier, *Codex B and its Allies, A Study and an Indictment*, 2 Vols., (London: Bernard Quaritch, Ltd., 1914), Vol. I, p. 415.

[2] Hoskier, *Codex B and its Allies, op. cit.*, Vol. I, p. 415.

[3] Hills, *The King James Version Defended, op. cit.*, pp. 106–112, 224–225, etc. This is Dr. Hills continuing theme throughout his works.

faith would always be wavering and we could never be confident that a dealer would not soon appear with something new from somewhere else. We would be wondering if the damming of the Nile River had destroyed some Greek text which would show us a new wonderful truth.

We already possess and have had all along the actual TRUTH of Scripture! We have, by faith in God's promises to preserve His Word, an assumed premise, a priori, of God's providential preservation of the text. Someone may say "prove it", but this fails to comprehend the nature of a priori premise. As Letis has reminded us: "One does not prove a first premise. A premise by definition is something one assumes, not something he proves".[1] And even more to the point – the context of these promises having been for the use of His people throughout time – we rest with maximum certainty that we already have those precious Words at our disposal as preserved in the Bible of the Reformation.[2] We are not lingering in expectation for the modern text critics to "restore" them to us.

It is not our position that the text found in the majority is the true text merely because it is found in the majority of mss (although some do so argue). It is the *reason* that this text is found present in the majority that is decisive. "The reason", says Letis, "that all defenders of the TR since the Reformation follow the majority text is because it reflects the actual text **historically used by the Church** – the believers in all ages to whom Jesus promised to lead into all truth – as sacred text".[3]

True, the supporting evidence such as that of Sturz' mentioned previously which revealed that the papyri sustained many of the Byzantine readings as being second century was encouraging, but our confidence is not in isolated scrapes of old papyri or vellum. It is founded on a much surer foundation. Our confidence is in God's never

---

[1] Letis, "A Reply to the Remarks of Mark A. McNeil" (Edinburgh: 9-3-1990), p. 2. This is a 5 page response to a 8-14-1990 appeal to Dr. Letis for documentation from Mr. Eldred Thomas. Mr. Thomas' TV program on the subject of Biblical texts had aired resulting in Mr. Mark McNeil's having taken issue with him on several particulars.

[2] Hills, *The King James Version Defended, op. cit.*, pp. 224–225.

[3] Telephone conversation with the author, October, 1989. Dr. Letis has contended the same many times in various articles and correspondence (also Dr. Hills, *King James Version Defended, op. cit.*, p. 113). He so does in "A Reply to the Remarks of Mark A. McNeil" (Edinburgh: 9-3-1990). *Vid. supra*, footnote 1, page 79.

failing promises and in the text which has been continuously in public usage by the Church. This is why the *Textus Receptus* is the true text, not merely because of its great statistical "superiority" or "probability". To not grasp or comprehend this leaves the reader with a "tentative" Bible. Even opponents freely admit this conclusively decisive point. For example, Professor Kurt Aland forthrightly grants:[1]

> "It is undisputed that from the 16th to the 18th century orthodoxy's doctrine of verbal inspiration assumed ... [the] *Textus Receptus*. It was the only Greek text they knew, and they regarded it as the 'original text'".

Merrill M. Parvis penned:

> "The *Textus Receptus* is not the 'true' text of the New Testament ..".

but then incredulously went on to concede:[2]

> "It [the TR] was the Scripture of many centuries of the Church's life. ... **The *Textus Receptus* is the text of the Church**. It is that form of text which represents the sum total and the end product of all the textual decisions which were made by the Church and her Fathers over a period of more than a thousand years." (author's emphasis)

These candid admissions by such leading scholars of the opposing view underscore and prove our entire thesis – that the *Textus Receptus* always has been the NT used by the true Church!

Indeed, this has recently been conclusively proven by a remarkable piece of new manuscript evidence. Three tiny fragments of uncial codex which were acquired in Luxor, Egypt in 1901 and donated to Magdalen College in Oxford, England had been preserved in its library in a butterfly display case. Dated c.A.D. 180–200 in 1953, both sides of the Magdalen Papyrus (the largest piece is 1⅝" X ½") exhibit Greek script from the 26th chapter of Matthew.

In 1994, these fragments came to the attention of the German biblical scholar and papyrologist Dr. Carsten Peter Thiede (Director of the Institute for Basic Epistemological Research in Paderborn, Germany).

---

[1] Kurt Aland, "The Text Of The Church?", *Trinity Journal 8* (Fall 1987): p. 131.

[2] Merrill M. Parvis, "The Goals Of New Testament Textual Studies", *Studia Evangelica 6* (1973): p. 406.

Painstakingly re-dating the scraps, Dr. Thiede placed them at A.D. 66 – the only known first century NT text extant.[1]

But this was only the beginning. Using an eipflourescent confocal laser scanning microscope, Dr. Thiede found that fragment 3 (recto) revealed the TR/KJB reading from Matthew 26:22, "*hekastos auton*" – every one of them – rather than "*heis hekastos*" – each one [in turn one after the other] – as all the various critical texts read![2] Thus this A.D. 66 fragment now documents the antiquity of the TR/KJB text to the time of Peter, Paul, John the Apostle, as well as some of the 500 witnesses of our Lord's resurrection (I Cor.15:4–8).

Neither should it be imagined that Dr. Thiede was motivated to arrive at these conclusions because he is a TR supporter; he is not. As a papyrologist and having hard physical data in hand, he was not intimidated to abandon his new textual discoveries because they conflicted with the presuppositions and conjectural theories of New Testament textual scholars. Facts, you see, are stubborn things.

Further, when we use such phrases as "the Word of God says ...", "the Scriptures say ..." or "the Holy Bible says ..." etc., we do *not* merely mean the Hebrew Masoretic text and the Greek *Textus Receptus* (Syrian, Byzantine, Traditional Text, or majority text). We are refer-ring to something contained between the covers of one Book, something that we can hold in our hands as English speaking laymen or elders. We are speaking of an entity which we can read daily for our own edification and read aloud to our families, friends, and Church. That "something" is known as the Authorized or King James Bible. We proclaim without reservation that it is the Holy Spirit guided, absolutely faithful English translation and rendering of God's original

---

[1] Carsten P. Thiede & Matthew D'Ancona, *Eyewitness to Jesus*, (New York: Doubleday, 1996), pp. 124–125. Dr. Thiede's findings appeared in a sensational front-page story of the December 24, 1994 (Christmas Eve) edition of the London *Times*.

[2] Thiede, *Eyewitness to Jesus, op. cit.*, p. 59–60. These results were presented at the 21st Congress of the International Papyrologists' Association in Berlin August, 15, 1995, and met with "unanimous approval" (p. 61). Dr. Thiede adds that the precise nuance cannot be rendered in English. The Magdalen text emphasizes they were all speaking at once – a realistic portrayal of a dramatic moment with its accompanying excitement. But the standard critical text reads such that they spoke one after the other, waiting their turn in an orderly fashion (p. 60). Thus this original reading which was always preferable based on internal criteria is now corroborated by the oldest papyrus of Matthew's Gospel (p. 60).

wording. As such, it speaks to us as final authority (in context) against which all matters must be measured and tested. It is "THE" Bible, the living Words of the Living God – it is the Word of God.

THE MODERN VIEW OF INERRANCY
AMONG MOST CLERGY

The current vogue in conservative, fundamentalist scholarship will come as a great surprise to the layman. Today, most conservative Protestant clergymen have been brainwashed as mere youths in their late teens or early twenties at the various denominational Bible colleges and seminaries concerning the doctrine of inerrancy of Scripture. As a result, when most of these pastors etc., declare that they believe in the verbal, plenary inspiration and/or inerrancy (or some other similar declaration of faith in the Scriptures) what they really mean is that only the original autographa were inerrant. Now this is devastating, as we have no originals preserved for our use. But the situation is even worse than that, for neither do the vast majority of these men believe that the text contained in the original autographs has been preserved intact. That is, they have been taught as very young men that for hundreds of years many original readings have been lost to the Church.

They have also been taught, hence most subscribe to the teaching, that these lost readings are in the process (and have been so for the past one hundred years) of being *restored* back to their pristine original forms by the use of modern textual criticism techniques and methods. Thus, if we were to ask one of the scholars representing this school of thought whether he could show us the "infallible Word of the Living God", he would take us to his private study – wave his hand toward between 800–1200 books on his library shelves and reply that somewhere contained within all those volumes exists the Word of God. He would inform us that the problem was very complex, but all was well as he and other brilliant scholars were working on putting the puzzle back together. Besides, he would assure us, no major doctrinal issues are in doubt in the meantime.

If we pressed these men further to better define their position, we would discover that very few believe that there exists on the earth today between two covers such that it could be held in the hand – the Bible. That is, in their opinion, is that which they hold in their hand having the words "Holy Bible" inscribed thereon and read from the pulpit to their flocks, the inerrant Word of God? If they were honest, regardless of the version to which they personally subscribe, the answer would be "NO"!

THE CONCLUSION OF THE MATTER

The fact is that nearly everyone who invokes "the autographs" does so to alter (and thus pervert) the Providentially preserved Scriptures. Most men and/or institutions that claim to embrace the "Doctrine of Inerrancy", do so intending it to apply only to the "originals". In so doing, they have embraced Benjamin B. Warfield's perverted version and definition of "inerrancy". Such men and/or institutions lay claim to faith in "inerrancy", but have no doctrine of Providential Preservation and thus they are still – sad to say – looking for (or attempting to restore) the inerrant autographs. It is deceitful for pastors to hold high the Bible and proclaim "I believe God's Word is inspired from cover to cover" while saying under one's breath, "in the autographs". To maintain that we must have the autographs today in order to be certain of the text is as imprudent and needless as to insist that we require the cup from which Christ drank before communion can be rightly celebrated.[1]

Thus, whereas we aver and asseverate that the "originals" were "inspired" (Greek = θεοπνευστος = theopneustos = inspired by God or God breathed) and inerrant, we cannot subscribe to the modern version of the "Doctrine of Inerrancy" as it embodies only the "originals" whereas it excludes Providential preservation of the original text. This new form of the "Doctrine of Inerrancy" must be recognized by the Church as un-scriptural, untrue, tainted, prostitute, and depraved – a Canaanite idol – as it, in its current Warfieldian form, holds only to a non-existent entity.

Moreover, it is MADNESS to attempt to attain something that one already has as his possession. Hours upon wasted hours of study and research have methodically been carried out, not only by lost apostates and liberals, but – sadly – by brilliant conservative fundamentalists attempting to produce that which we have had as our deposit all along – the infallible, inerrant Word of the Living God, as He Himself

---

[1] Robert D. Preus. *The Inspiration of Scripture, A Study of the Theology of the Seventeenth Century Lutheran Dogmaticians*, 2nd ed., (Edinburgh: Oliver & Boyd Ltd., 1957), p. 49. Preus is citing Dannhauer.

promised. Oh Christian, gird up the loins of your mind – make bare the arm!

The truth is that the maligned *Textus Receptus* has been the base with which B tampered and changed; the church at large recognized this until the year 1881 when Hortism was allowed free play.[1] Those who accept the Westcott-Hort text, or its modern counterpart, are placing their faith upon an Egyptian revision which occurred somewhere from 200 to 450 A.D. and was abandoned by Bible believers all over the civilized world between 500 to 1881 A.D.[2] After the true Church buried B and its allies through disuse, these Egyptian "mummies" were "resurrected" in recent times and re-stamped as "genuine". Thus, the modern Church has accepted as authentic that which the early Church rejected. Such are the ways of present day Laodicea (Rev.3:14–22).

It must be kept in mind that when God promised to preserve the text against permanent destruction, He did not guarantee within that promise the accuracy of each and every manuscript. Although this certainly could have been done, it would have necessitated a continuing miracle. Moreover, God's promise did not include the threat of His immediate execution of the person causing an error or corruption in the copying or production of a manuscript, whether deliberate or accidental. His promise merely guarantees the preservation of the text. And this He has done over the centuries through the vehicle of the true Church.

The excuse that we needed a revision because older manuscripts had been found has been exposed as unfounded and untrue. Beyond all question the fact is that the *Textus Receptus* is the dominant Greco-Syrian text from 350 to 450 A.D.[3] Since these dates go back to the time of the production of *Vaticanus* B and *Sinaiticus* א, why is the authority of these two spurious MSS always being flaunted by reason of their supposed superior age?

Biblical scholars working in concert with publishing companies, neither of which answer to any ecclesiastical authority within the

---

[1] Hoskier, *Codex B and its Allies, op. cit.*, Vol. I, p. 465.

[2] *Ibid.*, p. 468.

[3] John Burgon, *The Traditional Text of the Holy Gospels Vindicated and Established*, ed. Edward Miller, (London: George Bell and Sons, 1896), pp. 116, 121.

Church, have taken the Bible away from the people. Through their endless writings and promotions, they have convinced many in the community of believers, pastors included, that only they can truly appreciate and understand the Bible. They infer that they are the only ones who can determine what it means. Does not this arrogance resemble a giant leap back to the Catholic position from whence the Reformation sprang? Did the dauntless Reformers work, endure persecution and die in vain?

Moreover, the single greatest move of the hand of God since the time of the Lord Jesus and the Apostles as recorded in the Book of Acts was that of the Reformation. This great move must be recognized as the direct result of the historical restoration by Erasmus of the true text that the Apostles lived and wrote under the inspiration of the Holy Spirit. The reader must then confront himself with the question: "If the Reformation were the fruit of restoring to the people the text known today as the *Textus Receptus*, where is the great revival that should have accompanied the labor of the past 100 years of text-critically editing and correcting that document?" The "Great Awakening" of the 1700's as well as the revivals of the late 1800's and early part of the 1900's under men such as Wesley, Whitefield, Finney, Spurgeon, Moody, R.A. Torrey, and Billy Sunday were all preached from the King James text.

To the contrary, we know of no revival that resulted from using the critical text. Thus we see that the *fruit* of the TR/KJB has been the harvest of millions of souls. In stark contrast, the fruit of the critical text and its offspring has been doubt, division, endless debate, wasted time and energy that could have been spent in worship or evangelical effort, and the destruction of the faith at most seminaries and many pastors along with the sheep who feed at their feet. If the critical text is the better text, where are the great revivals that should have followed this enterprise? Does not this hard historical truth bear irrefutable testimony as to which text the Spirit of God has endorsed and stamped genuine – to that which He breathed man-ward?

The next question is, which of the versions – if any – reflects the original wording from the autographs in English? Without hesitation, we say that the King James "Version" is that entity. It is "the Bible" in the English language. Yet strangely when this and the overall message contained in this manuscript has been shared and explained by the author (as well as by others, present or past), the reaction from the vast majority of readers or listeners – whether laymen, pastors or professors – has been so bewildering and unexplainable. Not seeming to comprehend that help and warning are being offered rather than "criticism", most become very defensive and often irritated. A pall of apathy overshadows the subject. This is indeed a troubling tragedy in the extreme.

Yet, as things stand we are left in the strange circumstance whereby everyone is permitted and encouraged to come to the religion classroom, Bible study, Sunday School class, Church service, etc., all bearing different "textbooks". Such is never tolerated or practiced in any other learning situation. University professors of English, Chemistry, Physics, Mathematics, History, etc., do not permit such a practice for they well know the chaotic situation that would result. An atmosphere for real learning would not exist in such an environment. Even the authorities in the lower levels of education – the High Schools, Junior Highs, and Elementary schools – know better. No, the institution selects the textbook (whether good or bad), and the student purchases it. Other material relevant to the subject are to be found and utilized in the reference area of the institution's library. It would seem that only within the confines of the Christian Church is such foolishness practiced and tolerated. Yet in so doing, have we not completely set aside all common sense and logic?

What difference does it all make? Not only do we have the confusion caused by two rather different competing forms of the Greek text, but one of them (the eclectic text) incorporates errors and contradictions that undermine the doctrine of inspiration and invalidate the doctrine of inerrancy. The other (the Traditional majority Text) does not. The first is based on subjective criteria, applied by liberal critics; the second is based on the consensus of the manuscript tradition and actual usage by the true followers (the real Church) down through the centuries.

Because the conservative evangelical schools and churches have generally embraced the theory (and therefore the presuppositions) that underlies the eclectic text (UBS[3] &/or Nestle[26]), there has been ongoing compromise or defection within the evangelical camp with reference to the doctrines of Biblical inspiration and especially inerrancy. The authority of Scripture has been greatly undermined; no longer does it command immediate and unquestioned obedience. Consequently, there is a generalized softening of our basic commitment to Christ and His Kingdom. Equally dismaying, through our missionaries we have exported all of this to the emerging churches in the "third world". Alas! Truly, the ancient landmark is being removed (Prov.22:28)!

What then shall we do, throw up our hands in despair? Indeed no! With God's help let the people of God work to undo the damage. We must start by consciously making certain that all our presuppositions, our working assumptions, are consistent with God's Word. If we approach the evidence – the Greek MSS, patristic citations, ancient versions and most especially, God's many promises to preserve His Word – if we acknowledge the fact that the faithful have used the *Textus Receptus* as their NT down through the years as retained to this day by the Greek Church; we will have a credible, demonstrable basis for proclaiming and defending both the inspiration as well as the inerrancy of the New Testament text.

We *have* a compelling basis for total commitment to God and His Word. The trumpet has been clearly sounded (I Cor.14:8). Whom will you believe? What will you do?

Heaven and earth shall pass away:

but my words shall not pass away.

Mark 13:31

BIBLIOGRAPHY

Aland, Kurt. "The Text Of The Church?," *Trinity Journal 8* (Fall, 1987): page 131.

Aland, Kurt. "The Greek New Testament: Its Present and Future Editions." *Journal of Biblical Literature*, LXXXVII (June, 1968): p. 184.

Burgon, John William. *The Traditional Text of the Holy Gospels Vindicated and Established*. ed. Edward Miller. London: George Bell and Sons. 1896.

Burgon, John William. *The Last Twelve Verses of the Gospel According to S. Mark*. Oxford and London: James Parker and Co. 1871.

Burgon, John William. *The Last Twelve Verses of the Gospel According to S. Mark*. Introduction by Edward Freer Hills. Ann Arbor, MI: The Sovereign Grace Book Club. 1959.

Burgon, John William. *The London Quarterly Review*. (October): 1881.

Colwell, Ernest Cadman. *What is the Best New Testament?* Chicago: Chicago UP. 1952.

Colwell, Ernest Cadman. "The Origin of Texttypes of New Testament Manuscripts." *Early Christian Origins*. ed. Allen Wikgren. Chicago: Quadrangle Books. 1961.

Encyclopedia Britannica. Vol. 16. 1936.

Eusebius, of Caesarea. *Ecclesiastical History*. Vol. 1. The Loeb Classical Library. trans. by Kirsopp Lake. Cambridge, MA: Harvard University Press. 1980.

Fuller, D. O., ed. *Which Bible?* 3rd ed. Grand Rapids, MI: International Pub. 1970.

Green, Jay P. (ed.). *Unholy Hands on the Bible*. 2 Vols. Lafayette, IN: Sovereign Grace Trust Fund. 1990. Volume I includes the complete works of John William Burgon, Dean of Chichester.

Hills, Edward F. *The King James Version Defended*. 4th ed. Des Moines, IA: Christian Research Press. 1984.

Hoskier, Herman C. *Codex B and its Allies, A Study and an Indictment*. 2 Vols. London: Bernard Quaritch, Ltd. 1914.

Hoskier, Herman C. *Concerning the Text of the Apocalypse.* 2 Vols. London: Bernard Quaritch, Ltd. 1929.

Jones, Floyd Nolen. *The Septuagint: A Critical Analysis.* 6th ed., rev. Houston, TX: KingsWord Press. 1998.

Jones, Floyd Nolen. *Which Version is The Bible.* 17th ed. revised & enlarged. Houston, TX: KingsWord Press. 1999.

Kenyon, Sir Frederick G. *Our Bible And The Ancient Manuscripts.* 5th ed. London: Eyre & Spottiswoode. 1958.

Letis, Theodore P. *Edward Freer Hill's Contribution to the Revival of the Ecclesiastical Text.* unpub. M.T.S. Thesis. Emory University. 1987.

Letis, Theodore P. "A Reply to the Remarks of Mark A. McNeil." Edinburgh, Scotland: Sept. 3, 1990.

Moorman, Jack A. *Missing in Modern Bibles.* Collingswood, NJ: Bible For Today Press, # 1726. 1988.

Moorman, Jack A. *When The KJV Departs From The "Majority" Text.* Collingswood, NJ: Bible For Today Press, # 1617. 1988.

Moyer, Elgin S. *Who Was Who in Church History.* Chicago, IL: Moody Press. 1962.

Musurillo, Herbert. *The Fathers of the Primitive Church.* New York: Mentor-Omega Pub. (Nihil Obstat) 1966.

Newman, Albert Henry. *A Manual of Church History.* Vol. I. Valley Forge, PA: Judson Press. 1902.

Parvis, Merrill M. "The Goals of New Testament Textual Studies." *Studia Evangelica 6* (1973): pp. 397 & 406.

Pickering, Wilbur N. *The Identity of the New Testament Text.* Nashville, TN: Thomas Nelson. 1977.

Pickering, Wilbur N. *What Difference Does It Make?* Dallas, TX: n.p. 1990.

Preus, Robert D. *The Inspiration of Scripture: A Study of the Theology of the Seventeenth Century Lutheran Dogmaticians.* 2nd ed. Edinburgh: Oliver & Boyd Ltd. 1957 (1955).

Radmacher, Earl & Hodges, Zane C. *The NIV Reconsidered.* Dallas, TX: Redencion Viva Pub. 1990.

Ray, Jasper J. *God Wrote Only One Bible*. Junction City, OR: Eye Opener Pub. 1980.

Reumann, John. *The Romance of Bible Scripts and Scholars*. Englewood Cliffs, NJ: Prentice Hall. 1965.

Sturz, Harry A. *The Byzantine Text-Type And New Testament Textual Criticism*. Nashville, TN: Thomas Nelson. 1984.

Thiede, Carsten P., and D'Ancona, Matthew. *Eyewitness to Jesus*. New York: Doubleday. 1996.

Tyndale, William. *Tindale's Triumph, John Rogers' Monument*, The New Testament of the Matthew's Bible 1537 A.D. John Wesley Sawyer, ed. Milford, OH: John the Baptist Printing Ministry. 1989.

Waite, D.A. *Defending the King James Bible: A Four-fold Superiority*. Collingswood, NJ: Bible For Today Press. 1992.

Wallace, Foy E. *A Review of the New Versions*. Ft. Worth, TX: Noble Patterson Pub. 1973.

Ward, Norman. *Perfected or Perverted*. Grand Rapids, MI: Which Bible Society. n.d.

Westcott, B. F. and F. J. A. Hort. *Introduction to the New Testament in the Original Greek*. New York: Harper and Bros. 1882.

Zuntz, Gunther. *The Text of the Epistles*. London: Oxford University Press. 1953.

INDEX

Mark 16:9-20, 48, 52, 68, 69, 72, 73
Martyr, Justin, 69
Marx, Karl, 66
Mary, the mother of Jesus, 62, 65
McNeil, Mark A., 79
Miller Edward, 76, 84
Minuscules (mss/cursives), 67
Moody, Dwight L., 63, 85
Moorman, J.A., 1, 71, 75
Moyer, Elgin S., 63
Mussolini, Benito, 66
Musurillo, Herbert, 63

Neo-Platonism, 63
Neutral Text, 75
Nestle, Eberhard, 39, 47, 53, 67, 72, 86
Newman, Albert Henry, 63

Origen, Adamantius, 62-66, 69

P-66, (Bodmer II Papyri), 74, 76
Pantaenus, 63
Papias, 69
Papyri, Bodmer II (P-66), 74, 76
Papyri, Chester Beatty, 74, 75
Parthenos, 62
Parvis, Merrill M., 80
Passover, 9, 60
Paul the Apostle, 56, 62, 68, 75, 81
Peshitta, 57
Peter, Simon the Apostle, 56, 58, 80, 81
Pickering, Dr. Wilbur N., 55, 68, 69, 73, 75, 76
Plato, 63
Plenary Inspiration, 82
Preus, Robert D., 83
Providential Preservation, 78, 79, 83

Radmacher, E., 53
Received Text (TR), 39, 40, 47, 53, 57, 58, 66, 67, 71-73, 78-81, 84, 85, 87
Reformation (ers), 47, 57, 58, 68, 79, 85
Reincarnation, 64
Reumann, John H.P., 63
Revision Committee (1881), 71

Saccas, Ammonius, 63

Scrivener, F.H.A., 76
Septuagint (LXX), 62
Sinaiticus Aleph, 39, 40, 66, 68, 69, 71, 73, 84
Spurgeon, Charles Haddon, 85
Stephens (Stephanus 1550), 47, 57
Sturz, Harry A., 74, 79
Sunday, Billy, 85
Syrian Text (Byzantine), 39, 57, 71, 74-76, 78, 79, 81, 84

Tatian of Assyria, 69
Textus Receptus (TR), 39, 40, 47, 53, 57, 58, 66, 67, 71-73, 78-81, 84, 85, 87
Thiede, Dr. Carston Peter, 80, 81
Thischendorf, C. von, 69
Thomas, Eldred, 79
Titus of Rome, 25
Torrey, R.A., 85
TR (*Textus Receptus*), 39, 40, 47, 53, 57, 58, 66, 67, 71-73, 78-81, 84, 85, 87
Traditional Text (T.T.), 39, 57, 60, 68, 75, 76, 81, 84
Transmigration of the Soul, 64
Trinity, 65, 80
Tyndale, William, 57

United Bible Society (UBS), 39, 47, 53, 67, 72, 86

Vaticanus B, 58, 66, 69, 71, 73, 78, 84
Verbal Inspiration, 72, 80, 82

Waite, Rev. Dr. D.A., 53, 66, 67, 71
Waldenses/Waldensian, 57
Wallace, Foy E., 62
Ward, Samuel, 53
Warfield, Benjamin B., 83
Wesley, John, 70, 85
Westcott, B.F., 39, 53, 58, 66, 67, 68, 71, 72, 75, 76, 77, 84
Western Text, 71, 74, 75, 78
Whitefield, George, 85

Zuntz, Gunther, 74